More than a Whistle Stop

Janelle Wootton McQuitty

*Featuring snapshots
of life in a mid-twentieth century railroad village
and other old railroad photos*

Books by Janelle Wootton McQuitty

No Time to Quit, Pioneer America Seen through the Life of Rocky Mountain Man
   Uncle Dick Wootton
Rocky Mountain Man, large print

More than a Whistle Stop

Published by Janelle Wootton McQuitty, LLC
Farmington, New Mexico, United States of America
2018
ISBN-13: 978-0-9988385-3-3

Dedicated to my parents,
Mr. and Mrs. John P. (Johnnie and Eileen) Wootton, Jr.
who made Lamy, New Mexico, my childhood home
Photo February 1958

Thanks

For railroaders, teachers, family, and townsfolk of mid-century Lamy, New Mexico.

To Jack McQuitty, Sr., for permission to use some of his more recent photos, so noted.

To Jean Campion, Lin Harris, Ruth and Witt Harwell, Myles Lark and Christine Mahannah, Jack McQuitty, Sr., Judy Wootton Mendez, and Don Snell for critiques or consultation

Contents

Preface

My father died at sixty years of age. Except for a few remembered stories, his wealth of history died with him.

Someday someone may want to know what it was like to live in a mid-twentieth century railroad village. I originally intended to make a booklet of photos with added captions; but, when I inquired if anyone wanted more information, I was encouraged to include oral history and some basic facts.

This book is an oral history, written, a pictorial history of life in the mid-twentieth century railroad village of Lamy, New Mexico. It is not intended as a complete history of the village, not even a complete oral history, but as slices-of-life; for many paragraphs know more stories, more details.

Although I have an antipathy for revisionist history, I understand that different people viewing the same incident or time period would remember and record different aspects.

I arrived in Lamy, New Mexico, on an Indian Detours bus. A newborn, I was carried home to a Santa Fe Railroad converted-boxcar home, east of the depot. Having lived there nine months previously, I was then ten days old. My mother spent ten days in the hospital after my birth, fourteen days after my older sister's, and four days after my younger brother's. Those were standard hospital stays after childbirth at the time. Dad was working freight; so Aunt Mary came from Maxwell, New Mexico, and accompanied us home. Neither my aunt, nor my mother drove.

Except for almost one year, the school year of 1948-1949, I lived in Lamy until mid-January 1959. The foundation of my life formed there.

Snapshots and memorabilia are primarily from the mid-twentieth century; those not of that time period are noted.

Lamy is not situated due north-south. To say northwest, southwest, etc. would be cumbersome to the reader; so I say north, south, east, or west, which will give the reader direction. I prefer directions of left and right, but left and right depend upon one's point-of-view.

In cases which may refer to either male or female, the masculine pronoun may be used in the old style to refer to either without any offense intended.

I wish I had a photo of each mid-century resident and a good picture of each structure, but I give you what I can.

Janelle Wootton McQuitty

Photos on the previous page:
Top right: John Wootton, Jr., early 1970s
Bottom left, Janelle Wootton, 1950
Front cover, Amtrak engine, Lamy, New Mexico, August 2018, photo by Jack McQuitty, Sr., used by permission

Lamy, New Mexico

*L*amy was a railroad village, not a village that had a railroad. It was a village because of the railroad—the Santa Fe Railroad.

In the great years of nineteenth century railroad expansion, Cyrus Holliday conceived the idea of building a railroad line that would replace the old Santa Fe Trail, whose commerce had financially strengthened the young United States since 1821. Holiday planned to follow the Santa Fe Trail from Kansas to Santa Fe, the capital of New Mexico Territory. He began on a small scale with a shorter name, but the name Atchison, Topeka, & Santa Fe Railway defined his aim. As it turned out, the railroad would go far beyond his original goal and build an empire, but neither Atchison, Kansas, nor Santa Fe, New Mexico, would be on the mainline.

The Atchison, Topeka, & Santa Fe Railway (A.T. & S.F.), better known as the Santa Fe, chugged up and across Uncle Dick Wootton's Raton Pass on the Colorado-New Mexico border on December 7, 1878. It arrived in Las Vegas, New Mexico, with fanfare on July 4, 1879, and built on toward Santa Fe, New Mexico. Laying track in the high altitude country near Glorieta, New Mexico, made some laborers sick; they were sent to the hospital in Santa Fe to recover. Ties continued to be laid in place and rails spiked down until rails reached a point the A.T. & S.F. called Galisteo Junction, about eighteen miles from Santa Fe. The grade into Santa Fe, New Mexico, wasn't feasible for mainline rail service. Plus, by that time, the Santa Fe Railroad had far-reaching plans toward Mexico and the Pacific Coast.

Residents of Santa Fe, New Mexico, passed a $150,000 bond issue for construction of a spur/branch line between Santa Fe and the mainline at Galisteo Junction. On February 9, 1980, the first A.T. & S.F. train arrived in Santa Fe; and

 the Santa Fe Railroad continued laying tracks toward points south and west. In Galisteo Junction, the railroad built a two-story, wood depot in1880, a water tower, and a coal chute for its steam powered locomotives. In the picture on the left, railroader Claude Hawkins and John Wootton III stand near the coal chute, 1953.

On or by January 6, 1881, little Galisteo Junction was officially renamed Lamy in honor of Archbishop Jean Baptiste Lamy, who had come to Santa Fe, New Mexico, from France.

In its early days of American occupation, begun in 1846, New Mexico Territory included present-day New Mexico and Arizona, as well as parts of other western states. Without enough manpower to enforce law and order in the entire region, New Mexico attracted many with less than love-your-neighbor values. In some places, like nearby Las Vegas, New Mexico, hooligans found bi-vocational life beneficial: outlaw by night and law-abiding, working citizen by day, or vice-versa, as was convenient. New settlements provided new opportunities for outlaws.

For a short time, Lamy was as close to a wild west town as any child of the 1940s or 1950s would hope to see; cowboys and the West were popular themes for children of the mid-twentieth century. Using their imaginations, children played in the dirt, among the piñon trees, and climbed hills pretending to be a part of the wild west without knowing what had taken place in their own hometown 50-60 years previous. In Lamy's early years, the Santa Fe County Sheriff made several trips out to tame things down; and, within a few years, Lamy had shaped up into a nice little village.

At the time Lamy came into being, many settlements were cropping up as Americans moved westward—villages based on farming, ranching, mining, or railroading. Each village built its own community according to what the citizens wanted and were willing to build. In Lamy's early years, there had been two boarding houses, saloons, two hotels, and stores. Lamy kept it simple: no opera house, no public library. In 1909 the railroad replaced its original wood depot with a new Mission Revival style depot close to the center of town. That became the permanent Lamy Depot.

Lamy Depot with Lamy Mountain in the background, 1990s
Photo by Jack McQuitty, Sr., used by permission

Note the changes to Lamy Depot in the above picture
from the following picture of Lamy Depot in 1950.
Pictured left to right:
Joe G. Wootton, Stella Fram Wootton and her husband, Bill L. Wootton,
all of Las Vegas, New Mexico.

Mainline tracks near the depot, Lamy, New Mexico, August 2018
The mainline of the Atchison, Topeka, & Santa Fe Railway
stretches from Chicago to Los Angeles.

The Railroad

The Santa Fe, officially the Atchison, Topeka, & Santa Fe Railway, was the best known American railroad in the mid-twentieth century. Its mainline track linked the country from Chicago to Los Angeles; but a transportation map of mid-twentieth century America shows Santa Fe rails branching like blood vessels to nurture the nation, providing transportation for passengers, freight, and mail.

The Santa Fe Railroad had been such an essential part of the nation's World War II effort from 1941-45 that its employees were deferred from military service to keep trains transporting troops, military supplies, and home front needs. The draft board reassessed each man every six months to determine whether the highest need for his service was at home on the rails or in military service. If an employee volunteered or was drafted for military service, the Santa Fe held that railroader's slot in the seniority roster. After the war, those who returned to rail service had their seniority as though they had never been absent.

NOTICE OF CLASSIFICATION App. not Req.

John　　　　　Peter　　　　　Wootton

(First name)　　　(Middle name)　　　(Last name)

Order No. __291__ has been classified in Class __2-A__

(Until __June 28__, 19__44__)

(Insert date for Class II-A and II-B only)

by ☒ Local Board.
　☐ Board of Appeal (by vote of __3__ to __0__)
　☐ President.

__January 31,__ 19__44__　　　*J. J. Shumaker*

(Date of mailing)　　　(Member of local board)

The law requires you, subject to heavy penalty for violation, to have this notice, in addition to your Registration Certificate (Form 2), in your personal possession at all times—to exhibit it upon request to authorized officials—to surrender it, upon entering the armed forces, to your commanding officer.

DSS Form 57. (Rev. 3–29–43)

Railroaders worked long, hard hours—sometimes twelve to sixteen hours a day—until the strike of 1950. I watched the picket. I knew the men walking, holding signs. Even before the strike, they came to drink coffee with daddy in our home across the street from the depot.

When the strike came, my brother had just turned one; my sister was in second grade at Lamy School; Mama had laundry and cleaning and dishes to do. That left

6

me, almost three and a half, to sit on Daddy's lap, dunk my toast in his coffee, and hear our friends discuss the strike. During the strike, trains were run by railroad officials and a few employees who crossed the picket line to work. Railroaders called them scabs. I knew they didn't mean the kind you pick off of your knee after a fall. If my friend's didn't like scabs, neither did I (right). I stood in our yard across the road from the depot and watched the men walk the picket line.

The strike brought about better conditions for employees, especially better work hours. There were times after strikes in subsequent years that railroaders thought some union-required conditions were a bit nit-picky; however, lines had to be drawn somewhere. For instance, a passenger crew was within 20 miles of their destination when they had worked the prescribed maximum hours allowed according to the Union and railroad agreement. The train had to stop; so the crew could be relieved by a fresh crew; the relieved crew then rode to the same destination.

The Santa Fe Railroad story is an adventure of its own—progress interrupted by the Civil War, struggles for finances, races for right-of-ways, expansion, receivership, and stabilization.

From its inception, the Santa Fe endeavored to be more than another railroad in the nineteenth century's up-cropping of upstart railroads. Conceived in the era of Manifest Destiny, the Santa Fe's founders endeavored to do its patriotic part in national expansion. As it expanded, the Santa Fe advertised the West throughout the United States and Europe. Its first advertisements were for settlers, like wheat farmers who settled on the plains of Kansas. At one period, the Santa Fe offered free transportation to those who would migrate and settle along its mainline. By the same token, when the great grasshopper raid hit Kansas and Colorado, the Santa Fe provided free transportation for some who couldn't afford to stay.

The Santa Fe Magazine

Battleship Texas
Pride of Our Navy

May 1917

The A.T. & S.F. continued to encourage patriotism. On the previous page is pictured the cover of the July 1917 *Santa Fe Magazine*, published during World War I. Below is a page from the May 1917 issue encouraging employees to do their part in the nation's war effort.

HOW YOU CAN "DO YOUR BIT"

The Santa Fe attracted tourists to the Southwest, promoting not only the Southwest's unique landscape, but also attracting attention to the crafts and skills of the American Indian, now known as Native American. The Santa Fe and Fred Harvey had joined hands to provide enjoyable dining, both on trains and in Harvey Houses at various places along the Santa Fe line. Each Harvey House had its individual décor. Each offered fine dining with meticulous service in a relaxed atmosphere. Harvey Houses were built, not only in convenient locations for dining and rest, but often as a gateway to further Western adventure.

Harvey offered employment for men and women of high moral character only. Many young men and women from throughout the nation moved to the Southwest to take advantage of employment opportunities with the Harvey system, and many remained in the area and became an asset to the nation's new communities

A Fred Harvey dining car arrived in Lamy in January 1881 and opened for business the next month. Years later, Lamy's El Ortiz—the smallest Harvey House—was built on the east lot adjacent to the depot (on the left as one faces the depot). William Jennings Bryan, "Buffalo Bill" Cody, and author Owen Wister, considered the father of western fiction, were among El Ortiz's famous guests in early years; but Harvey's littlest house drew clientele from many walks of life. They came for a meal, for a night, or for an extended stay. Wister said of El Ortiz, "This little oasis among the desert hills is a wonder of taste to be looked back upon…, and forward to…. The temptation was to give up all plans and stay a week for the pleasure of living and resting in such a place." (Poling-Kemps, 1989, 120, 121) El Ortiz closed before the United States joined World War II and was torn down in 1943. The Santa Fe planted a spacious lawn in its place.

John Wootton, Jr. at the site of the blasted coal chute

Lamy's coal chute and water tower supplied coal and water for A.T. & S.F. steam engines, which were used on the mainline and continued to be used on the branch line from Lamy to Santa Fe until about 1953. The train which used the branch line was called the Branch; I don't know if it had a more official name. After the Branch quit using steam engines, the Santa Fe blasted and buried the coal chute, c1954. Dad went to the site to take movie pictures. Mama and we kids climbed a hill and sat and watched the coal chute tumble into the hole prepared for it. The coal chute had been a landmark to us on our way home from trips to Santa Fe or Las Vegas, New Mexico. We were almost home if we could see the coal chute.

The railroad kept extra engines in Lamy in readiness for freight trains that needed one or more helpers to cross nearby Glorieta Pass.

The Santa Fe and Its Employees

In the 1930s the Santa Fe Railroad had a doctor in Lamy—Dr. Francis Marion Crume. We all heard about Doc Crume, but he died in 1938; so we didn't know him. As far as I know, Lamy never had another resident doctor after Dr. Crume left. His wife outlived him until 1965, but I never knew her. They are both buried at Sunset Memorial Park in Albuquerque.

The Santa Fe also built hospitals for its employees'. Lamy's nearest hospital was on Central Avenue in Albuquerque, New Mexico. It had large spacious grounds, with lawns across its rolling slopes until the hospital property was reduced as city growth progressed. My sister, brother, and I played on the rolling slopes when our parents visited our grandpa. Dad and Mama went there for surgeries. Both my father and his dad died there.

The A.T. & S.F. established reading rooms to enrich employees' minds. At least as far back as the early 1900s, the railroad published a monthly employees' magazine. It included national, as well as international news—often involving transportation in some manner, news of employees or their families from towns all along the line—provided by local employees, obituaries, jokes, cartoons, poetry, history, and ads—like the one on the left. The magazine had a definite team spirit approach. On the left is a portion of a watch ad during World War I. On the following page is the cover of the July 1916 issue of *The Santa Fe Magazine*.

The Santa Fe Magazine

July 1916

In the early days of railroads, railroading was a dangerous career—lost limbs, lost lives. The Santa Fe had a strong safety emphasis. Even the birthday cards they sent employees, as seen on the following pages, encouraged the person to be safe and stay around for another year.

Note the Santa Fe emblem with plans for progress into the twenty-first century.

The fronts of three birthday cards and the back of one
The little boy is Chico, seen in many A.T. & S.F. publications and promotions.

The Santa Fe not only encouraged safety,
but also commended employees for safety.
Note the Santa Fe's little safety icon: Axy Dent. The company was ever on the
move to wipe him out.
I had forgotten his name; thanks to Evan Stair and G.J. Perez for remembering.

THE ATCHISON TOPEKA & SANTA FE
COLORADO DIVISION
SAFETY CERTIFICATE

Mr. J. P. Wootton _____ worked as

Conductor _____ the entire

year of __1966__ without an incident of personal

injury.

_____

Santa Fe   C.B.Kurtz

Superintendent

The Santa Fe also considered the need for housing. There wasn't much rental property available in villages and small towns In smaller places, like Lamy, the Santa Fe built homes—usually frame houses or converted-boxcar-houses and charged a minimum rent. This made housing available without a railroader needing to buy and resale a home, which was important because of the railroad's seniority/bumping option. Jobs were held on seniority, as well as a classification, basis. For instance, engineers and firemen were in one class, brakemen and conductors in another. If an employee wanted another position in his class, he could bump another person with less seniority out of that job. That person, in turn, had to bump another person. It wasn't a personal thing, just the way the system operated; it was done all the time. Railroaders' time books listed the divisions, the breakdown of each division, and the name of every employee according to rank and hiring date, examples follow.

CONDUCTORS — THIRD DISTRICT
New Mexico Division — July 1, 1947

No.	Name	Date Brakeman	Date Conductor
1.	Peters, H. A.	3- 7-06	1-25-10
2.	Byers, W.	12-30-16	2-24-17
3.	Smiley, A. H.	5-29-13	11-16-17
4.	Ludwig, F. N.	1-17-15	11- 3-19
5.	Zinn, P. R.	6- 6-15	11- 5-19
6.	Mallory, W. R.	7-14-15	11- 8-19
7.	Squires, M. W.	5-21-16	11- 9-19
8.	Bruington, G. H.	6-24-16	11-10-19
9.	Burke, C. E.	9-28-16	12- 1-19
10.	Maloney, J.	11-16-17	12-22-19
11.	Newcomb, W. O.	8-16-16	6-23-20
12.	Thompson, T. D.	12- 6-16	8-10-20
13.	Notgrass, E. W. (Abs)	12-26-16	8-23-20
14.	Becker, A. C.	1- 2-17	9-20-20
15.	Zumbro, J. W.	6-22-17	4-25-25
16.	Stumpf, A. C.	10- 6-17	9- 1-28
17.	Shriver, W. L.	9-26-19	9-11-28
18.	Johnston, C. E.	11- 3-19	9-14-28
19.	Line. W. L.	2-20-20	9-16-28
20.	Davidson, R. A.	5-14-25	12- 7-35
21.	Raney. C. E.. Jr.	7-10-25	12- 9-35
22.	Wootres, J. W.	9- 8-25	12-10-35
23.	Ferguson, K. S.	3-24-26	12-13-35
24.	Smith, R. L.	10-19-26	7-10-41
25.	Short, C. F.—8 a.m.	3-28-31	7-30-41
26.	Kirkendall, F. L.—10 a.m.	3-28-31	7-31-41
27.	Wilcox, W. H.	3-29-31	8- 1-41
28.	Alka, H. R.	4-28-31	8- 2-41
29.	Kincaid, C. A.	8-17-35	6-28-43
30.	Dovel, F. M.	9-16-35	7- 1-43
31.	Casick, J. M.	7-26-41	12-16-45
32.	Sojka, H. P.	10-19-41	12-18-45
33.	Jacobsen, C. J.	1-28-42	12-24-45
34.	Wooton, J. P.	6- 9-42	12-28-45
35.	Harris, H. L.	6-27-42	12-31-45
36.	Lee, J.	8- 9-42	1- 8-46
37.	Elterman, F. L.	8-31-42	1-11-46
38.	McIntyre, J. F.	9- 2-42	1-12-46
39.	White, R. L.	9-12-42	1-15-46
40.	Leatherman, A. E.	6-22-42	12-31-46

Conductor and Brakemen seniority lists above and on the following page were published in the Railway Employees Seniority List Time Book, Issue of Santa Fe 1948.

BRAKEMEN — THIRD DISTRICT
New Mexico Division — July 1, 1947

No.	Name	Date Brakeman
1.	Baker, A.	6- 6-09
2.	Burks, G.	11-16-10
3.	Van Hook, V. B.	11- 8-13
4.	Zirhut, W. J.	4- 1-18

Brakement — Third District — Continued

No.	Name	Date Brakeman
5.	Bartley, G. O.	6- 9-39
6.	Foster, L. C.	10- 5-41
7.	Romaine, T. H.	11-18-41
8.	Williams, M. A.	1- 6-43
9.	Kimball, P. E.	1-30-43
0.	Erxleben, W. P.	10-24-43
1.	Albers, M. L.	12- 9-43
2.	Kepley, O. L.	12-19-43
3.	Gates, R. L.	1- 8-44
4.	Coppock, D. L.	4-20-44
5.	*Nesbit, H. R.	4-20-44
6.	Rainey, T. A.	4-25-44
7.	McAnulty, O. R.	4-26-44
8.	Shearmire, J. L.	4-29-44
9.	Kimbrel, J. E.	2- 1-45
0.	Bowman, C.	2- 3-45
1.	Plotner, E. A.	2-19-45
2.	Lee, E. E.	3-24-45
3.	Allen, H. L.	6-14-45
4.	Napps, W. O.	6-21-45
5.	Juul, C. N.	6-26-45
6.	Machalek, J.	10- 3-45
7.	Connell, R. W.	11-20-45
8.	Ruley, R. R.	12-13-45
9.	Price, R. D.	12-14-45
0.	Regensberg, C. C.	12-31-45
1.	Rumley, C. A.	6-21-46
2.	*Griffin, J. D.	7-12-46
3.	Howell, F. A.	7-25-46
4.	Nelson, A. H.	9-07-46
5.	Rogers, R. W.	9-24-46
6.	Healey, R. F.	10-31-46
7.	Jones, W. F.	11-22-46
8.	Hinkle, R. C.	12-10-46

*Absent.

The Engineer and Firemen Seniority List on the following page is from a pamphlet of seniority lists compliments of Personal Finance Co. of Albuquerque, New Mexico, 1945.

17

Official Seniority List of
Engineers and Firemen—Third District
New Mexico Division—January 1, 1945

NAME	Seniority Date As Fireman	Seniority Date As Engineer
Trainer, W. J.	8-31-1901	6- 1-1905
Trainer, L. C.	5-15-1905	5- 5-1910
Anderson, H. E.	5-11-1907	7- 3-1911
Sundt, J. M.	12-15-1908	1-11-1913
Carvill, T. J.	3- 6-1910	7-12-1916
Mortsching, W.	6-15-1911	9-17-1916
Moulton, W. G.	9-30-1910	11- 6-1916
Sulier, A. M.	7-25-1911	11- 7-1916
Stanley, A. H.	4-21-1912	2-14-1917
Slaughter, N. R.	9-28-1912	7- 1-1917
Vansickle, N. G.	6- 3-1913	12- 9-1917
White, H. E.	12-29-1913	12- 9-1917
Beeler, E. H.	10-30-1915	5-29-1920
Cook, H. J.	6-25-1916	10-10-1923
Niehans, A. A.	12-16-1916	10-24-1936
Shaum, J. R.	1-22-1917	11- 2-1936
McGuire, W. H.	5- 5-1917	11- 3-1936
Brann, H. C.	6-13-1917	11- 8-1936
Welch, E. W.	6-24-1917	1-28-1937
Thomas, J. B.	8-31-1917	10-29-1939
Thornburgh, J. S.	3-17-1918	8-22-1942
Lindenberger, C. T.	1- 7-1920	11- 6-1942
Edmonds, G.	7-16-1920	11-25-1942
Frank, P. E.	11-15-1922	11-26-1942
Pitt, S. D.	12- 7-1922	12- 9-1942
Compton, C. A.	7-20-1923	12- 9-1942
Dyche, R. F.	11- 1-1923	1-12-1943
Fletcher, G. D.	11-21-1923	2- 4-1943
Scarbrough, J. S.	1-26-1924	3- 4-1943
Jones, H. F.	7-30-1924	12-17-1943
Hawkins, C.	11- 9-1925	12-17-1943
Roberts, L. M.	7- 1-1926	4-12-1944
Belcher, R. J.	9- 9-1926	12-10-1944
Malone, J. L.	9-24-1926	12-26-1944
Schutt, E.	12-18-1926	
Boyce, J. W.	11- 9-1928	
Murphy, J. B.	6-30-1937	
Raybun, J. L.	7-16-1937	
Owings, J. B.	6-11-1942	
Sanders, J. B.	8- 4-1942	
Hunter, L. E.	8- 6-1942	
Bryant, G. L.	8- 9-1942	
Miller, C. T.	8-24-1942	
Post, F. Y.	11- 7-1942	
Thompson, D. A.	11-15-1942	
Tanner, L. R., Jr.	1- 6-1943	
Bates, N. M.	1- 8-1943	
Rodgers, Ben	1-11-1943	
Worf, R. E.	2-12-1943	
Koons, G. A.	3- 9-1943	
Wootten, W. L.	3-15-1943	
Ingham, J. W.	9- 9-1943	
Spohr, S. F.	9-12-1943	
Dettman, E. W.	10- 2-1943	
Kellogg, G. M.	10-26-1943	
McGuiness, E. L.	10-30-1943	
Sandy, H. C.	10-30-1943	
Coble, H.	1- 1-1944	
Simpson, R. F.	1- 6-1943	
Nichols, E. L.	1-16-1944	
Cawthorne, C. J.	1-21-1944	
Everett, T. G.	4-11-1944	
Chellew, T. J.	6- 3-1944	
Chapman, J. R.	8-27-1944	
Mullins, E. W.	11- 9-1944	
Smith, A. J.	11-15-1944	
Hassler, L. D.	11-30-1944	
Irvin, T. F.	12- 2-1944	
Boyer, C. F.	12-12-1944	
Fast, P. B.	12-23-1944	

The Santa Fe gave its employees and their dependents a free railroad pass. Because the Santa Fe Railroad worked together with the Indian Detours bus company, which transported passengers from the Lamy depot to Santa Fe, railroaders and their dependents also had a pass for bus rides.

In one's early years of service, a railroader applied for a pass each time he wanted to ride the train. He received a pass for a specific destination, example on the right. After a number of years the employee was given a pass within a specified district. Permission

THE ATCHISON, TOPEKA & SANTA FE RAILWAY SYSTEM
Not Good on No. 7

Pass _____ October 19, _____ 19 37 _____ No.
(Name Removed) 000----
Good only on Western Lines, and P. & S. F. Ry.

Account B&B Helper
Good until Nov. 15 19 37 When Countersigned by
Countersigned:
A. T. DAVID
President

To Lamy, N. M. From Raton, N. M.

Address Las Vegas

Requested by HEW Issued by HRM
Conductors will punch pass below as honored, final conductor cancelling and taking up pass when honored to destination.

O	O	O	O	O	O	O	O	O	O	O O O
1	2	3	4	5	6	7	8	9	10	Cancel

only need be applied for if the desired destination was beyond that district.

After more years of service, an employee received an open pass to be used any time, any place on a Santa Fe passenger train, example below. At all times; however, a pass was limited to certain passenger trains. They were only for the common-man's trains, like 23 and 24, 7 and 8. Passes were not for the Chief or Super Chief.

Years later, after Amtrak took over passenger service, most passenger trains were

Original pass was yellow; in black & white, the Santa Fe insignia shows. Corners were rounded.

THE ATCHISON, TOPEKA AND SANTA FE RAILWAY SYSTEM
1969-1972   B- 10887
Pass Mr. (Name Removed.)
Conductor.

BETWEEN ALL STATIONS UNTIL DEC. 31, 1972, UNLESS OTHERWISE LIMITED BELOW AND SUBJECT TO CONDITIONS ON BACK

VALID WHEN COUNTERSIGNED BY S. S. ROSE, R. G. YOUNGKAMP OR SAM OWEN
COUNTERSIGNED
President

taken out of service; so passes could be used for seats on the higher class trains; however, one had to apply for a pass for a specific time period and call to make seat reservations the day before departure. The seat could only be reserved after the train passed through the boarding station the day before one wanted to depart.

Passes were railroad specific; however, railroads honored employees of other rail lines by giving a discount. For instance, when our family traveled in 1955, we rode the Santa Fe as far as we could and then connected to the Southern Pacific to reach our destination. Mama said we paid a penny a mile per person on the SP.

When we visited Disneyland in 1958, people purchased a book of tickets for a set number of rides; the entrance fee didn't include rides. However, the Park honored Dad's Santa Fe pass on their area-themed, miniature Santa Fe Railroad trains in each of the park's four theme areas. The Santa Fe & Disneyland Railroad train cars were 5/8 scale reproductions of early Santa Fe trains. We used our tickets on other rides and appreciated not having to walk so much within the Park.

On passenger trains, a dining room steward walked through each coach car announcing each meal at least twice. He announced the dining room was serving and the last call for that meal. Mama packed lunches for our train trips; we never ate in the diner.

We enjoyed the newsboy's trips through the cars, offering sandwiches, snacks, newspapers, pillows, and trinkets. He returned to his stand in one of the cars. Sometimes we children walked back to his stand and bought something. He packed a lot of interesting things in a small space.

On a passenger train, if our family was able to get seats next to one another—one pair of seats in front of the other, Dad would ask for the front set to be turned; so we could face one another. Santa Fe passenger trains were known for their ample leg room.

Railroad personnel dressed clean, neat, sharp—whether working passenger or freight, wearing suits or bib overalls, they wore pressed clothes and polished shoes—polished to a sheen for passenger service. At one point, Dad paid my brother to polish his shoes. After my brother wiped and polished the shoe, I'd put my foot in the shoe to give it stability as he brushed and buffed. Even passengers dressed pressed. Mid-twentieth century America was not a sloppy-go-lucky nation.

Competition and loyalties among railroads of the era could be likened to that of professional ball teams at the end of the century. Among U.S. railroads, the Santa Fe was the winning team. It didn't go for an A in service and safety for everyone involved; it went for an A+, and Santa Fe families knew it.

In a day when many corporations had been and still were out for their own good, the Santa Fe had its eye out for their employees and customers—both passenger and freight, as well as for the company. Sure, there was a bit of "them" and "us" between blue and white collar workers; but, they were a team. As in a family, it was okay to talk about one another, but not okay for someone from the outside. The Santa Fe's white collars led behind the scene; blue collars were players on the field—on the train itself, in service shops, on bridge gangs; line, rail, or signal repairmen; in depots—and in various types of service, as in the railroad's hospitals.

A. T. & S. F. OFFICIALS
Western Lines

G. C. JEFFERS
General Manager — Amarillo

W. L. MORE
Assistant General Manager — La Junta

J. E. LESTER
Superintendent, Colorado Division — Pueblo

W. H. JONES
Superintendent, New Mexico Division — Las Vegas

J. F. CARTER
Asst. Superintendent, N. M. Division — El Paso

P. J. DANNEBERG
Mechanical Superintendent — La Junta

R. M. CHAMPION
Trainmaster, Colo. Division, 1st District — La Junta

J. H. BLAKE
Trainmaster, New Mexico Division — Las Vegas

E. W. NOTGRASS
Trainmaster, New Mexico Division — Las Vegas

R. D. SHELTON
Trainmaster, Colo. Division, Pueblo District — Pueblo

W. D. BLACK
Road Foreman of Engineers, Colo. Division — La Junta

O. E. KINNEY
Road Foreman of Engineers, Colo. Division — La Junta

J. B. MERRIT
Road Foreman of Engineers, New Mexico Div. — Raton

W. W. LYONS
Master Mechanic — La Junta

This list of officials was included in the Santa Fe Railroad's Employees Seniority List Time Book, Issue of Santa Fe 1948.

Each year trainmen had to pass the Santa Fe rules and regulations exam.

Form 1691 Std.

THE ATCHISON, TOPEKA & SANTA FE RAILWAY SYSTEM.

Mr. J. P. Wootton

has passed satisfactory examination on the rules, operating department, and is qualified

for service as Conductor

Signature of Employee

Colorado
Division

Examiner

Oct. 26 1961

Form 1691 Std.

THE ATCHISON, TOPEKA & SANTA FE RAILWAY SYSTEM.

Mr. J. P. Wootton

has passed satisfactory examination on the rules, operating department, and is qualified

for service as Conductor

Signature of Employee

Colorado
Division

Examiner

Nov. 13 1962

"Santa Fe."

RULES AND REGULATIONS.

OPERATING DEPARTMENT.

Every three months each trainman was required to have his pocket watch checked and certified by a Santa Fe Railroad approved watch inspector. The watch didn't have to be cleaned that frequently, but it did have to be certified accurate. A railroader was required to carry his watch certification at all times. With such fine watches the trains ran on time or thereabouts—more often thereabouts.

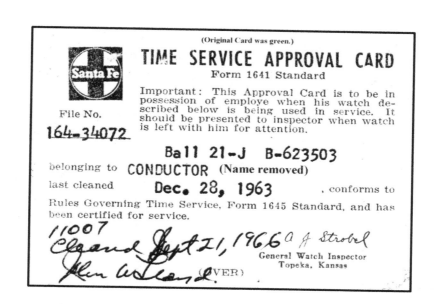

TIME SERVICE APPROVAL CARD

Form 1641 Standard

Important: This Approval Card is to be in possession of employe when his watch described below is being used in service. It should be presented to inspector when watch is left with him for attention.

File No.

164-34072

Ball 21-J   B-623503

belonging to **CONDUCTOR** (Name removed)

last cleaned **Dec. 28, 1963** , conforms to

Rules Governing Time Service, Form 1645 Standard, and has been certified for service.

11007

Cleaned Sept 21, 1966 a A Strobel

General Watch Inspector
Topeka, Kansas

(OVER)

Lamy Specific

Trains whistled when they entered a populated area, whistled when they left. In Lamy we were more accustomed to the sound of a train than to the ring of a telephone. In the 1950s there were only three telephones in the entire village: one at the depot, one at the store, and the other at the saloon. If a call came to the depot, someone there would relay the phone message—on foot—to any place in town. We didn't need phones; word got around in a personable way. In Lamy we saw train signals and the hand signals of conductors, not traffic lights, not even street or traffic signs—except one stop sign. We knew to watch the lights on train signals and to pay attention to the rails themselves when crossing tracks.

We knew the rumble underfoot as we stood on the platform waiting for a Warbonnet (Santa Fe passenger engine) to come into the block. The redcap would pull his big luggage/freight wagon from the depot toward the track. With its wooden bed, long wooden handle, and large, iron-rimmed and wooden-spoked wheels, it could have belonged to any railroad era. One of the station agents stood on the platform holding a long rod, shaped like a Y with a long base. Tied with string between the ends of the Y were orders for trainmen. The agent held the rod high; so the trainman could grab the stringed message off of the rod as the train passed the agent. There was no computerized contact. Messages were relayed to the agent by telegraph, the agent to the trainman—without stopping the train.

As the train spushed steam and eased to a stop (Some might say it puffed to a stop; but it really sounded more like a long, slow s-p-uuu—sshh!), the red cap pulled his wagon across the brick-paved platform and stopped in front of the baggage car. The baggage man slid the double-wide, baggage car door open, and the men began loading luggage and freight onto and off of the wagon.

The conductor opened the coach car, stepped down, and placed a metal step stool on the platform. He offered his hand to passengers as they stepped down, out of the train. Other passengers stood on the platform waiting to board the train. Some trains had reserved seats; so passengers went to the coach in which their seat was located. For trains with unassigned seats, like 23 and 24—the Grand Canyon Limited, the conductor would ask the passengers their destination and direct them to the coach car they should board. Once all passengers boarded, the conductor signaled the engineer "All aboard," picked up his stool, stepped in, and closed the door.

67618 M

IMPORTANT
KEEP IN SIGHT
If you change
your seat please
carry this
with you.

Trip tab

It was rather nice not to have assigned seats because when a passenger in your coach car reached his destination, his seat was open. If you liked his seat better than yours, you could take your trip tab from its slot above your seat, insert your tab in the holder above his seat and enjoy the view from your new seat.

Some passengers who arrived in Lamy were greeted by people waiting for them. Others purchased tickets to ride an Indian Detours bus into Santa Fe. They boarded the bus parked in front of the depot. Once the bus left, the depot became silent, except for the clicking, ticking of the telegraph, sending and receiving messages of trains coming and going and of all that needed to be communicated concerning passenger and freight trains, baggage and freight. Two agents were in charge of Lamy Depot.

To a child the best part of the depot was the Chiclets gum machine near the track-side door. Several flavors of gum represented by their distinct color boxes were packed two per tiny, cardboard box. The depot was clean and well kept. Inside seats were wood with padded seats; outside there were smooth concrete benches in a portico—comfortable benches until decades later when the portico floor was changed. Rather than redo the floor, another layer of flooring was added making the benches squatty, with little leg room.

Passengers could enter the depot through one of three doors: from the north side –the road side—parking area where the Indian Detours buses parked, from the portico on the east side, or from the platform near the tracks.

The depot was roofed with California tile. Whether it had been re-roofed before or not, I don't know; but I know it was re-roofed in early 1952 because as Jimmy Turner and I walked to the post office, we remarked how nice it was be old enough to walk to the store by ourselves without having to hold anyone's hand. As we neared the depot, we saw workmen replacing tiles on the depot roof. Of course, back home our news was no news; both of our fathers saw the depot every day. His dad, Jess Turner, was the signal maintainer. They moved from Lamy cMay 1952.

Lamy was fortunate to have the main road paved from the highway turnoff clear to the depot. All other streets were dirt. Use had packed them well, but occasionally the county road grader drove up and down each one keeping them in good shape.

John Wootton III. Garage belonged to the signal maintainer.

Lamy seemed to get more rain and definitely more snow than Albuquerque to the south and less than Las Vegas to the northeast. Lamy did have some beautiful snows.

The mainline of the Santa Fe Railroad was built on the south side of Lamy Depot between the depot and Cerro Colorado. We sure didn't know the mountain by the name Cerro Colorado. We called it Lamy Mountain; but that's the name printed on maps. Pieces of pottery were scattered here and there on the top of the mountain—interesting connections to a people past. From a distance, the west side of Lamy Mountain looked like it had a giant ant hill on top. When I made that comment, I was told rock had been taken from there to construct the cathedral in Santa Fe. I don't know if that's the exact spot, but it is on record that rock was quarried in Lamy for use in building Santa Fe's St. Francis Cathedral. Much of that gravel-look has now weathered away.

Lamy Mountain and a portion of the mainline seen from the Lamy Depot, August 2018

The track on the north side of the depot was used by the Branch to switch freight cars, which traveled on the branch/spur track from Lamy to or from Santa Fe. From its establishment in 1879, Lamy was the key to passenger and freight service into Santa Fe, New Mexico, which had been a national destination since the inception of the Santa Fe Trail in 1821. In Lamy's early days, the railroad offered passengers the option to travel into Santa Fe on a small, spur-line passenger train. Originally, there was no charge for mainline passengers to ride to and from Santa Fe.

By 1929 there were only two passenger trains daily between Lamy and Santa Fe. Later the Branch combined freight and passenger service. By mid-century, the Branch was a freight train. Mainline passengers—or anyone, for that matter—could ride to Santa Fe, or from Santa Fe to Lamy, on Indian Detours buses, which met every passenger train that stopped in Lamy, except for trains 7 and 8, which were primarily freight trains—the fast mail trains—with a half a car for passengers; they came through Lamy at night. I don't know what the bus ride cost because we had a pass and never had to pay.

The Branch had seen heavy traffic during and immediately after World War II, but had settled down to strong and healthy by the late 1940s. The Branch hauled freight from the mainline in Lamy to Santa Fe and from Santa Fe back to Lamy.

The Branch serviced not only the Santa Fe Railyard, but businesses all along the track, as well as in and out of the state penitentiary, and to Bruhn's hospital.

After the War, many New Mexico servicemen who had survived the Bataan death march and subsequent years of servitude in Japanese prison camps were taken to Bruhn's Hospital in a recuperation effort. Many were so emaciated that the staff predicted they would not be able to have children or live more than five years. That was true for some; many did survive; some were able to have families. My cousin's uncle lived about five years.

In my adult years I learned that two of my school teachers were Bataan death march and prison camp survivors. They said nothing at the time, but thirty-five years after the war, one told me he had moved back to New Mexico because New Mexico understood Bataan survivors. I would like to have known more; but I respected him too much to pry. When I realized the other teacher was a Bataan survivor, I understood the reason he looked gaunt and had dark hollows around his eyes as long as I knew him, many years after his release.

Bruhn's Hospital was where Japanese men who had been released from the World War II Santa Fe internment camp boarded coach cars to return home via the mainline at Lamy. Before men were interned in Santa Fe, they had been examined and found to be a threat to the nation's security. All others were placed in other internment camps with their families until the end of the war.

Long after Dad died, Ray Ruley told me about those release-passenger trains on which he was brakeman and Dad was conductor in 1946. Surprised Dad never told me about them, Ruley laughed and told the story. On one of the internment trains, Dad turned to help the released internees. While his back was turned, one of them stole his conductor's suitcase with all his forms and reports. Ruley wasn't laughing now, "It was serious business; Johnnie had to report the incident to Chicago [Santa Fe offices]."

Ruley also told about the Branch hauling supplies for and from Los Alamos, New Mexico, the government's secret city for the World War II Manhattan Project. When the Branch hauled "Atomic cars" from Los Alamos, they knew nothing of the cars' contents. Mounted guards rode horseback alongside the train all the way to Lamy, where the cars were joined to a mainline train. Except for residents and approved guests, Los Alamos with its national scientific laboratories remained a closed city long after the War. Dad and Mama took us to see Los Alamos when it opened to the public in 1957.

One evening at supper, Dad told us they were going to electrocute a man at the penitentiary that night: did we want to go watch? None of us took him up on the offer. We did tour that old, stone pen one Sunday afternoon in 1958 when the state opened it to the public after prisoners had been moved to the new penitentiary. I remember the grounds, work buildings, women's building, and solitary confinement cells.

I have an alligator-skin wallet dad bought for me on one of his Branch trips into the pen when I was about six. Railroaders became personally acquainted with those along their service line because the city of Santa Fe wasn't big in the 1950s. A population sign on Cordova Road said 25,000 and some; I saw it most Sundays.

From time-to-time, we'd go with Dad to one of the businesses served by the Branch. At times he'd just stop in to say, hello, visit a little—a very New Mexico culture thing; sometimes he purchased items. Sometimes in the summer and on occasion after school, he'd take us along to the creamery where he bought ice cream by the 3-gallon, cardboard canister: one vanilla, one chocolate. To get to the cold storage freezer, we walked passed the ladies who were making popsicles and ice cream bars. The ladies all wore hairnets or caps. On one visit, the owner offered us a sample of his new watermelon ice cream. To me, it tasted nothing like watermelon. I think they only made it that year, and for good reason.

We frequently stopped at the produce company in the rail yard district. After a few minutes' visit, we'd walk with Dad and the manager, passed the front desk to the cold storage room with its boxes and crates of vegetables and fruits, and with its heavy vault-type door. I wasn't exactly afraid of the door, but I was always glad when we made it out without the door closing us in. It was a large, heavy thing, too heavy for a child to unlatch and open.

One dealer Dad knew distributed candy to small stores. We didn't keep candy on hand at home; but one year before we went on vacation, Dad took us to the candy man's house. He opened the back door of his truck—it seemed a little larger than a panel wagon, but not as large as an express truck. Boxes of candy lined each side, with a little walk way between. Dad picked a box of Heath Bars—Mama's favorite —and a box of Hershey's. Ordinarily, we had to save our allowance for candy. Mars and Almond Joy cost a dime each; all other candy bars, popsicles, packs of candy cigarettes, and five piece packs of gum cost a nickel. A penny could buy a piece of bubble gum or a sucker—unless it was a Tootsie Roll Pop; those were two cents. We seldom bought a bottle of pop. When we did, we three children divided it. Pop bottles required a deposit, refundable when returned.

John Wootton, Jr., on the depot freight platform, where the Branch tied up.
Bushes on the edge of the lawn, near the switching track, are tamaracks.
Next page: another view of the caboose tied up, 1955.

One day when I arrived home in Lamy on an Indian Detours bus, I noticed more cars than usual parked near the depot. When I got out of the bus, I saw several people I knew from Santa Fe. They told me they'd come to see the Queen of Greece, who was coming through on the incoming train. I ran home, told Mama, asked if I could take the movie camera to the depot, and hurried back—nothing new to our family. If need be, we could make it from our house to the depot when we heard a train coming. I arrived in time to take a picture of Queen Frederika. I knew nothing about her; but, to a child, a queen is a queen. Many people of Greek descent lived in Raton, New Mexico. We heard they turned out en masse to greet her and give her flowers; but it was dark by the time the train arrived in Raton. In Lamy, she stepped outside onto the rear platform of her car and waved to everyone; but she didn't make an appearance in Raton. News of their disappointment traveled down the tracks by word of mouth.

In my adult years I read that Presidents Grant, Hayes, and Roosevelt, and Generals Sherman and Sheridan, had been among early passengers who transferred from the train at Lamy on their way to Santa Fe. At one time in the 1920s, more than 500 people arrived in Lamy to transfer to Santa Fe to attend a convention. They waited in coach cars in Lamy until they could be transported to Santa Fe.

Railroaders dealt with people from all stations of life. In the mid-twentieth century, dignitaries, movie stars, politicians, artists, and scientists continued to pass through Lamy, whether traveling across the country or transferring on their way to Santa Fe, Taos, or Los Alamos. Politicians to Santa Fe, artists of the Taos-Abiquiu-Santa Fe art colony, scientists to national laboratories in Los Alamos all transferred at Lamy. One artist had trouble with his Lamy transfer. D. H. Lawrence had a home in Taos and wanted to be buried in Taos; but he died abroad. His ashes were shipped to his wife, who waited for him in Lamy. But, when the train showed up, he didn't. He was scheduled to be on the train, but it took twenty minutes to find him among the Indian Detours' passengers' baggage. Once he was found, the conductor gave the highball, and the engineer moved on. One seldom knows what all delays a train.

CHERYL CRAWFORD PRODUCTIONS

49 WEST 45th STREET, NEW YORK 19, N. Y. · LU 2-3466

JOHN YORKE, GEN. MGR.   WOLFE KAUFMAN, PRESS

April 16th

Agent, Lamy,
New Mexico.

Dear Sir:

This is to acknowledge that I received two items of personal
luggage at the Lamy depot Sunday April 6th.

I was manager with a theatrical attraction which toured
the United States this winter, and which was a heavy
customer with the Santa Fe Railroad. Through the courtesy
of the San Francisco office, my luggage was moved to Lamy.
I called the depot Saturday, April 5th and was told the
station was open 24 hours a day. When I came Sunday no one
was on duty at the station. Through the kindness of Mr. John
Wootton, a brakeman with the Santa Fe railroad, I surrendered
my tickets and obtained the luggage.

It has always been my experience in 15 years of railroading
attractions from coast-to-coast, that railroad men always rise to
meet any emergency, and, in this instance, the assistance
rendered to me by Mr. Wootton was in keeping with this fine
railroading tradition. Were it not for this unfailing courtesy
of all railroad personnel, many shows I have been with would
never have reached their cities in time.

Thank you,

Edwin R. Armstrong

PORGY and BESS ★ FAMILY PORTRAIT ★ ONE TOUCH OF VENUS ★ BRIGADOON
REGINA   ★   THE ROSE TATTOO   ★   FLAHOOLEY

A sample of railroaders' service.
The date Wootton helped was his son's birthday.

31

Lamy's railroaders were a mixture of nationalities; most were from various parts of New Mexico. Though one or two were first generation Americans, I think all were born in the United States. Besides the Branch crew, the Santa Fe employed other workers in the village, like the track supervisor and the signal maintainer, whose families lived side-by-side in Santa Fe homes.

Each weekday the track supervisor and the signal maintainer each rode the rails on an open, four-wheeled rail car while inspecting and maintaining signals and tracks. Their little motor cars had a little shed-type garage near the tracks in Lamy. The signal maintainer serviced signals between Waldo, New Mexico, and Glorieta, New Mexico. The signals were battery powered.

In this picture of McGinnis, his daughter, and their pit bull pup, the motor car garage can be seen on the left and the corner of Mallory's yard on the right. However, the picture was taken in the late 1960s; and the Mallorys had retired to Albuquerque by that time.

There were also two station agents and a red cap/call boy. Each morning the call boy walked to the home of each railroader, stood outside the bedroom window—or close enough to be heard inside, called the employee's name and announced the time he was to report for work. One morning in 1953, the call boy, a young Spanish man, called outside my father's window and then proceeded to call Dan Pitt, the railroader living in the efficiency apartment next door. We had recently been given a German shepherd dog when his owners moved away after closing their coach-car diner near the depot. Rover was a good dog and handsome, but we didn't know he was prejudiced. When the call boy walked to Dan Pitt's window, Rover followed, ran after him, actually; so, rather than stand outside the apartment and call, the callboy opened Dan's door and walked right into his bedroom-living room to announce the time he was to report for work. Come to find out, when Rover was a pup, he'd been mistreated by a Spanish man.

After that, of course, Rover couldn't run free. Using a long chain tied to a shade tree, Dad limited Rover's roving, yet gave him as much freedom as possible. Dad, but especially Mama, was a stickler for seeing to it that animals were well-cared for.

Dad bought a short, double-door storage unit from the railroad and made it a spacious house for Rover. Once in a while,

when they were going to be outside, one of my parents would let Rover run where they could watch him.

Although people in Lamy were a mixture of nationalities, Spanish was predominate. At that time, the majority of Spanish New Mexicans had roots in Spain, and wanted to be called Spanish Americans. New Mexico had been a Spanish colony of Spain and retained its name when Mexico took it from Spain in 1821. New Mexico was under Mexican rule only twenty-five years, and Spanish Americans in northern and central New Mexico were offended to be called

Mexicans. In 1846 New Mexico became a Territory of the United States. It remained a territory over 65 years before it was granted statehood in 1912.

We were taught manners and respect for others. As it was polite to call a person Spanish, it was also polite at the time to call a black person Negro; to call a person a nigger was as rude as calling a Spanish American a Mexican or greaser or calling a white person a gringo. The only Negroes/blacks most Lamy children saw were on trains. It was also polite to call American Indians, Indians. We didn't call them Native Americans because everyone who was born in America considered themselves native American. We knew American Indians weren't India Indians.

Perhaps Santa Fe County was ahead of its time or perhaps New Mexico had flown too many flags, been too long on the frontier edge to let something like skin color matter. To me, in saying Spanish American or American Indian, we were recognizing our roots, yet at the same time uniting as Americans, now belonging to the same nation. In some areas of New Mexico there were communities where people were leery of outsiders, some areas in which an outsider had better be careful; but in Lamy, I never knew nationality or color to matter to anyone except Rover, and he never showed prejudice to any of the neighborhood children who played with us, regardless of their skin tone.

Sure, people joked about others; but jokes weren't barbed. Oh, one can always find an individual who means ill and speaks ill; but in that era, jokes were comic relief, whether joking about a political party, a situation, a group, another person, or oneself. Every region and every group of people have a humor of their own, often not understood by others. Railroaders, especially the trainmen I knew, were a close lot with a distinct sense of wit and humor. Whether telling a joke or a story or pulling a practical joke, they didn't laugh at their own jokes, but had a big smile, an eye twinkle, or hearty laugh for those of others.

I especially remember the humor of John Casick, Ray Ruley, my dad, and a few who worked with them on the Lamy Branch and on passenger trains from Albuquerque, New Mexico, to La Junta, Colorado. Ruley laughed when he told of the year my parents bought three rubber masks for us children for Halloween. One was the face of a bald man with a distinct, long nose. He said Dad wore that on the Branch as their train switched on the rails in Santa Fe. When traffic stopped as the Branch went by, people in the cars stared at the long-nosed trainman.

Many were nicknamed. Ray Ruley liked his, which incorporated his initials, R.R.R.: "Railroad Ruley." Hawkins was "Hawk." I'm not sure Bob Belcher knew his, but his family is now gone; so it's okay to print "Baby Face."

Ruley and Dick Wootton—a Catholic and also a brakeman-conductor, both told me of the railroaders' cross. Catholics make the sign of the cross by touching their body and saying "In the name of the Father" (as they touch their forehead), "the Son" (touch their chest), "and the Holy" (touch one shoulder), "Ghost" (make a cross by touching the other shoulder). Railroaders used the same body signs as they said, "Atchison, Topeka, and the Santa Fe." The Santa Fe Railroad emblem, as seen below from an article in the July 1916 *Santa Fe Employees' Magazine*, is an encircled cross inscribed "Santa Fe."

The Santa Fe men didn't cross themselves as a type of worship, or as a mockery of worship. They were just loyal Santa Fe men, who thought it was clever. Their humor was not what would later be termed politically correct; in fact, humor of the era would not have been politically correct in the twenty-first century. But these railroaders were a people who had lived through the privations of the Great Depression and either the sorrows and hardships of War or the actual blood and guts of it. Oh, no. It's a wonder they laughed. No, no—as I said, one can always find a cruel one here and there in any place, any time; but these men weren't out to hurt one another with their humor. They laughed and raised us, the children of my generation, taught us, provided for us. They were responsible, respectful, hard-working men and women. They could have brought us up with bitter despair for all they had experienced—and some individuals did; but, as a whole, they peppered life with humor.

One day, Casick—just a few weeks retired, came to Albuquerque and stopped to visit Dad on his death bed before returning to his orchard in Embudo, New Mexico. The next day another railroader stopped by to see Dad, whose teeth were in a bedside container. The railroader told Dad, "Casick was down here yesterday looking for apple pickers without teeth."

Railroaders with an artistic inclination transformed their humor into caricatures, as seen on the next two pages. The first cartoon is of Johnnie Wootton, Jr. calling to John Casick when they were working on the Lamy Branch.

The Atchison, Topeka and Santa Fe Railway Company

OFFICE OF DIVISION SUPERINTENDENT
NEW MEXICO DIVISION

C. B. KURTZ,
Superintendent

W. R. BAKER,
Division Engineer

H. G. CRAWFORD,
Trainmaster

J. K. HASTINGS,
Trainmaster

Las Vegas, N. M.,
October 1, 1958

Mr. J. P. Wootton,
Conductor,
Lamy, New Mexico.

Dear Sir:

      Am advised that when it was necessary for us to cut two cars of cattle out of No. 31 at Spiess to unload for feed and rest, on September 27, you were on your layover at your home in Lamy at the time and volunteered to haul water with your own truck and equipment to Spiess in order to water this stock.

      Please accept the thanks of our management and the undersigned for your assistance in this emergency. It was about the only answer to the problem that confronted us and you may be assured that we appreciate very much the prompt and needed assistance.

Yours truly,

C B Kurtz

cc - Mr. J. K. Hastings
     Mr. E. J. Barnes (0-644 9-29-58)

SANTA FE—DEDICATED TO SERVICE

This letter, though it pertains to a railroad situation, typifies not only railroaders, but mid-twentieth century Americans, at least in New Mexico. Generally, if one knew another needed help, one pitched in and helped.

The following pages are pictures of Lamy trainmen.

Branch Crew, March 5, 1950: Engineer Walter McGuire, Fireman Mac McGinnis, Conductor John M. Casick, brakemen Johnnie Wootton, Jr., and Ray Ruley. Lamy, New Mexico.

Branch Crew: Johnnie Wootton, Jr., Cal Short, Bill Wootton, and Claude Hawkins

Branch Crew: Claude Hawkins, Bob Belcher, Bill and Johnnie Wootton

Trainman Jim Shearmire

rai

McGinnis

43

Railroad friends at the home of Walter Mallory one Sunday afternoon: Johnnie Wootton, Walter Mallory, McGinnis, and Alan Albin.

Derailments
& Accidents

On September 5th, 1956, about 3 a.m., the Santa Fe Chief collided with a mail train about five miles from Robinson, near Springer, New Mexico. A fireman threw a switch the wrong way, causing the oncoming Chief to collide with a mail train. Many were injured; twenty—all employees—were killed. I don't know where the Santa Fe took its wrecked engines, but they loaded them up and took them via the mainline to their destination.

They came through Lamy on a bright September afternoon after school. All of the neighborhood children went to the depot to see them close up. I didn't think I should go because I'd missed school. Dad understood, but wanted me to be able to see; so he took me to the higher ground behind Mallory's house to see it with him. I never thought then what that must have cost him to see the wreckage that had taken lives he knew. It was said that Shriver's knee cap was on the engine. Who could tell something like that? (W.L. Shriver is listed as number 17 on the Conductors' Seniority List on page 15.)

We heard many things about the wreck; but that knee cap story, the sight of the wreckage, and Dad and I seeing it together on that bright September afternoon remain with me. I have no pictures of that accident, nor of the wreckage that came through Lamy.

The photos in this section are of Lamy derailments.

The first five pictures are of a derailment at Lamy on November 2, 1948. The crew on that train was J. B. Murphey, Cook, C. F. Short, and J. P. Wootton, Jr.

A.T.&S.F. – Lamy, New Mexico
McQuitty Collection

Langford's son with Langford and Ingraham

A.T. & S.F. • Lamy, New Mexico
McQuiney Collection

Langford and son

John P. Wootton Jr.
A.T.&S.F. – Lamy, NM
McQuitty Collection

Brakeman Johnnie Wootton Jr.

48

Langford, Brakeman Wootton, and Conductor Cal Short. Notice the coal chute in the background.

The following pictures are of a derailment in Lamy in the early 1950s.

A.T. & S.F. ~ Lamy, NewMexico
McQuitty Ciollection

I amv children at the derailment site in I amv

A group of Lamy children inspect the derailment

Commerce

*L*amy commerce revolved around the Santa Fe Railroad, the primary employer. Lamy's population and village businesses had peaked by 1940. Now, in the mid-twentieth century, village businesses were reduced to a diner, two stores, and a saloon. The third building next to the mercantile store and the saloon stood vacant, except for storage. A traveling photographer used it once in the latter '40s. It may have had other occasional use.

Mr. Frank (Franscisco) Gonzales owned one of the stores. His store joined his home near the rear of the Catholic Church, on the right side as one faces the church. It was a welcoming little store like many village and neighborhood stores throughout the United States at the time. Because of World War II's rationings and needs, many families didn't have vehicles; so neighborhood stores within walking and carrying distance thrived well into the 1950s.

Many Lamy residents did their main grocery shopping in Santa Fe, where large grocery stores could offer better prices because they bought in bulk and didn't have as many middlemen to pay. Shoppers traveled from Lamy in one of three ways: on an Indian Detours bus, with a friend, or in their own vehicle. Most men did the family driving when they were off work because some women didn't drive. Mollie Lucero, Mrs. Boyce, Mrs. Smith, Mrs. Howell, Ruth Harwell, and some others did drive.

Leo Pick owned the general mercantile across from the depot; but Mr. Brown, assisted by Frank Villanueva, kept the store. Mr. Hanna had been the previous owner. It was an actual mercantile store with dry goods, groceries, paper goods, and other household items. On the left side of the store were the candy counter, the large, strong cash register, and the post office. Lamy's first post office opened in March 1881, served a short time, closed, and reopened in early 1884. My childhood memory stored no further details of the store's arrangement to the back, center, or other side—just a general picture of the merchandise and setting.

Summer 1950: Wootton children on the railroad lawn, formerly the site of Fred Harvey's El Ortiz. In the background: store-block and gas pump on the right, top of the Catholic Church just left of center, and Branch cars on the Branch track on the left.

The post office portion was complete with open mail boxes behind the counter, which only Mr. Brown and Mr. Villanueva accessed. It had a heavy metal, rectangular grill as seen in pictures of old banks and post offices. On that grill, two horizontal bars held a row of closely spaced vertical bars above the open space through which Mr. Brown handed the mail. All mail was general delivery, delivered to the post office from the depot across the street. A family member would go to the post office and ask the postmaster-storekeeper, "Is there any mail for <u>last name</u>?" He checked the small open mail boxes, where mail was filed alphabetically, and passed any mail through the opening below the grill.

From the time I was five, I walked to the post office. Each time I went alone, Mr. Brown put a piece of candy on top of the mail he handed me. If he gave me a pretty pastel covered coconut bonbon, I did not say, "I do not like coconut." Such rudeness didn't enter my thoughts. I said, "thank you," and took it home because my brother or sister would enjoy it. Of course, I ate any other. With thanks.

Mr. Brown's friend

I liked Mr. Brown; so when I overheard an adult say, "She's as slow as Mr. Brown," I didn't mind. One doesn't mind being like one's friend; besides, I hadn't yet learned to hurry passed little interesting things of life.

Mr. Brown died one summer night when I was six and a half. He went to bed, had not turned out his light, and never woke up. When he didn't come to work the next morning, Frank Villanueva went to see about him. Witt Harwell was called to pronounce him dead.

Mr. Brown had no family in Lamy; his family from Texas took him there for burial.

I was visiting my aunt at the time he died. When Mama wrote, she included news of Mr. Brown in her letter. I decided then and there I wanted to die like Mr. Brown.

Visiting with a Lamy neighbor who was an adult at the time, I mentioned Mr. Brown. My neighbor recalled him immediately, but not as I did. He said Mr. Brown was slow, sat in a chair, and would just look at him when he went into the store. He said Mr. Brown didn't seem to have much in the way of public relations skill. I asked my sister if Mr. Brown gave her candy with the mail. She said no, but she did remember that he'd given some old stock cookies to some of the school boys. They'd been eating them when one of the boys pulled one apart and found moths inside. Then the boys all had to take turns leaving the classroom to go to the bathroom. Each memory different from the man I knew.

After that, Frank Villanueva bought the store and moved it to the house across the street from the depot. Our family had lived in half of the house and the Villanueva family in the other half in 1950. Now the Villanuevas rearranged the living spaces into a store on the west side and a home on the east side of the house.

57

What had been our front porch became the entry to the store. Frank sold many of the same items, but he didn't stock dry goods. He sold Mobil gas with its flying horse icon and became the postmaster with a smaller version of the post office at the right rear of his store. He kept the little boxes in which to sort the mail and the heavy metal grate through which he also passed the mail. The glass encased candy counter was near his post office corner, the ice cream and soda pop cooler near the bay window at the front left (west). The cash register was on the right, near the front door. Shoestring potatoes, at twenty-five cents a can, were along the wall between the register and the ice cream—near the five cent Jack-Horner pies. You'd have to find the canned milk and crackers yourself; I can't help you.

We called many railroaders by their surname only. As a rule, children called most adults by Mr. or Mrs., plus their surname, but there were a few like Frank we called by their given names. By the time Frank had the store, I was old enough to realize his clientele included many train travelers. One summer day my friend and I were especially impressed by a large group of Shriners with their tasseled, red hats—such different attire and such vibrant red hats.

The saloon was not a place I knew like the store, but I knew those who did and had seen it inside and out. As was often the case in little towns, one man was known as the town drunk. I saw him passed out in front of the saloon as I walked to school when I was in first grade. Yes, I remember his name, poor thing. To a child the saloon was associated with the change of behavior its liquors brought to adults. The saloon became a more respectable place when it became the Pink Garter Saloon, about 1953. The Pink Garter was a supper club-saloon with fine dining (lobster, steak, etc.) and a distinct old West décor, which was in vogue. Local men could still get their drinks at the bar, but the Pink Garter attracted clientele from Santa Fe, Albuquerque, and surrounding areas. The clientele liberally plunked silver dollar tips down on the tables.

There had been a diner in a converted coach car east of the depot—between the lawn and the road. It closed in late 1952 or early 1953.

Summer 1950 view of the mercantile store and saloon from the railroad lawn
The rear of the diner can be seen at the far right, Wootton children forefront
Fire hydrant on edge of lawn

On the following page a group of children are pictured in front of the diner in 1950.

They are Mary Lou Gonzales, Susie and Ollie Jones—Susie with arms around Ollie, Betty Heatherly, Betty Salazar, Frances and Corine Sena, Janice Heatherly, Judy and Janelle Wootton with their dog Spot.

Besides Lamy stores and stores in Santa Fe, mail order companies were also available to Lamy residents. Catalogs were sent free upon request by companies like Montgomery Ward and Sears, Roebuck, & Co. Their Spring/Summer and Fall/Winter catalogs were thick. The Christmas catalogs were probably not more than ½" to ¾" thick. Postage wasn't expensive; so mail order shopping was convenient. A first class postage stamp cost three cents if the envelope was sealed. If the envelope flap was tucked inside, postage cost two cents. I don't know the official reason for that. People chose sealed rather than tucked when they wanted to ensure privacy or to include enclosures that might slip out of a tucked flap.

This page and the next show the front and back of a mail order catalog form.
Notice city zone, but no zip code on the address.

SEARS ORDER BLANK

Sears, Roebuck and Co., 3625 Truman Road, Kansas City 14, Mo. Date_____ 195____

WE GUARANTEE TO SATISFY YOU

PLEASE PRINT OR WRITE NAME AND ADDRESS PLAINLY
All members of the same household should order under one name

Please Do Not Write Anywhere In This Space

1
Name_____
(First Name)   (Middle Initial)   (Last Name)

Rural Route_____Rural Box No._____P. O. Box No._____
↰Please give both.↱

Street Address_____

Post Office_____State_____

2 HOW SHALL WE SHIP? (Mark X in Proper Square)
Parcel Post   Rail Freight   Express   Motor Truck
□   □   □   □
Name of Truck Line

3 SHIP TO ANOTHER ADDRESS? If you want this order shipped
to another person or to a different address, give directions here:

4 IF YOU HAVE MOVED since sending your last order, please give
your old address here:
Rural Route_____ Box No._____ Street Address_____
Post Office_____ State_____

CATALOG NUMBER	HOW MANY	NAME OF ITEM	COLOR Pattern, Finish, Initials, Etc.	SIZE Width, Length, Waist, Inseam	PRICE for Each, Yard, Pair, Etc.	TOTAL PRICE Add this column		SHPG. WTS. Add this column	
						Dollars	Cents	Lbs.	Oz.
077Y7023	1	jacket	blue preferred	12		3	49	1	10
38Y4221	1	nylon slip		34		2	49		07

	Total Pounds	Total Ounces

We are required by law to collect tax on sales for the following states:

If you live in Arkansas, Colorado, Iowa, Kansas, Missouri, New Mexico, Oklahoma or Utah, add 2c tax for every dollar's worth of goods you order.

TOTAL for Goods $_____

AMOUNT for TAX $_____

POSTAGE $_____

AMOUNT I OWE Sears on Previous Order $_____

TOTAL AMOUNT $_____

AMOUNT ENCLOSED { Sears Checks $_____ Money Order or Check $_____

TOTAL WEIGHT IN POUNDS

SEE OTHER SIDE FOR PARCEL POST, FREIGHT, EXPRESS AND TRUCK SHIPPING INFORMATION

IF THIS IS A CASH ORDER, CHECK HERE → □
and enclose remittance in full, including postage and tax, please.

IF AN EASY PAYMENT ORDER, CHECK HERE → □
and fill-in and sign the form on other side.

If you have an open account show account number here_____ At which Sears store?_____

Please be sure that you have given all necessary information such as colors, sizes

Printed in U.S.A. KF6088.1.5.51

K

WHEN ORDERING ON EASY PAYMENT TERMS THE HEAD OF HOUSEHOLD SHOULD SIGN BELOW AND ANSWER QUESTIONS

SEARS, ROEBUCK AND CO.: Enclosed is a deposit of $........which is to be used in part payment of the merchandise shipped. Beginning thirty days after the shipment is received, I will pay $........each month as required by your terms until the unpaid balance, plus carrying charge to be added as shown in your catalog, has been entirely paid. Until full payment is made, I agree that title to and right of possession of the merchandise shall remain in you, that I will not sell, remove, or encumber the same without your written consent, that I assume and shall be responsible for all loss or damage to said goods, and that upon default of any payment or payments, you may, at your option, take back the merchandise or affirm the sale and hold me liable for the full unpaid balance.

Signature of the Head of Household _____
(First Name)   (Middle Initial)   (Last Name)

Street Address _____
Please give both your Route and Box Number if on a Rural Route
Rural Route ___   Box No. ___

Postoffice _____   State _____   160

Have you had a previous Easy Payment Acct. with us? ___   What is account no.? ___   Is account paid in full? ___   Date final payment made? ___   At what Sears store? ___

If your account is paid in full or if you have not had a Sears account, please answer questions below

Age? ___   Married? ___   Number of Dependents? ___   Do you own your home? ___   Rent □ Board □   How much rent do you pay? ___

How long at above address? ___   Name of Landlord ___   Street Address ___   City and State ___

If less than 5 years at above address give former address ___   City and State ___

Are you steadily employed? ___   How long with present employer? ___   Occupation ___   Weekly Earnings $ ___

Name of Employer ___   Street Address ___   City and State ___

Name of your bank ___   City and State ___

If a farmer, how large is your farm? ___ acres.   How many acres under cultivation? ___

If you have any income in ADDITION to above, give amount and source ___

Give below the Names and Addresses of Two Stores With Which You Have Had Credit Dealings or Two Business Men Who Know You

Name ___   City ___   Business ___

Name ___   City ___   Business ___

The Spaces Below Are To Be Filled In When You Order Merchandise That Is To Be Attached to Your Property

Street number or other definite location of property in which material is to be installed ___   Cost of property $ ___   Amount of Mortgage $ ___

Name of person holding legal title ___   Name and address of mortgage holder ___

SHIPPING INFORMATION

PARCEL POST SHIPMENTS: On all articles for which you pay shipping charges, the shipping weight is given in the catalog description. Enter the total shipping weight for each article in the shipping weight column of the order blank. Add the pounds and ounces, then change ounces to full pounds (16 ounces equals 1 pound), and enter total weight in pounds. The postoffice counts fractions of a pound as a full pound and charges postage accordingly. For example: If your order totals 9 pounds and 34 ounces, allow postage for 12 pounds (34 ounces equals 2 pounds and 2 ounces, therefore 2 pounds 2 ounces plus 9 pounds equals 11 pounds 2 ounces).
Refer to postage chart above. If you live in Zone 3 or within 151 to 300 miles from Sears Mail Order House, the amount of postage to allow for 12 pounds is 46c. If you send more money than is actually needed to ship your order, we will refund every penny not used.
Complete ordering information can be found on the green pages in Sears General catalog.

PARCEL POST RATES Total Shipping Weight	Within City where Mail OrderHouse is located 151 Miles	Zones 1 and 2 Up to 151 Miles	Zone 3 151 to 300 Miles	Zone 4 301 to 600 Miles	Zone 5 601 to 1,000 Miles
9 ounces to 1 pound	10c	12c	13c	14c	15c
1 pound 1 oz. to 2 pounds	11c	15c	16c	19c	21c
2 pounds 1 oz. to 3 pounds	12c	17c	19c	23c	27c
3 pounds 1 oz. to 4 pounds	13c	19c	22c	28c	33c
4 pounds 1 oz. to 5 pounds	14c	21c	25c	32c	39c
5 pounds 1 oz. to 6 pounds	15c	23c	28c	37c	45c
6 pounds 1 oz. to 7 pounds	16c	25c	31c	41c	51c
7 pounds 1 oz. to 8 pounds	17c	27c	34c	46c	57c
8 pounds 1 oz. to 9 pounds	18c	29c	37c	50c	63c
9 pounds 1 oz. to 10 pounds	19c	31c	40c	55c	69c
For Each Additional Pound, Add	¾c	2c	3c	4½c	5½c

Above Parcel Post rates are subject to change without notice

FREIGHT OR EXPRESS SHIPMENTS: It is not necessary to send money to pay for freight and express shipping charges in advance. You pay shipping charges to agent at your freight station when goods are received. However, if there is *no agent* at your freight or express station, please include additional money with your order to prepay shipping charges. While express is faster, freight is the most economical way to ship heavy, bulky merchandise. Before marking method of shipment on order blank, compare freight and express rates shown on green pages of Sears catalog.

TRUCK SHIPMENTS—All Trucking Companies do not make deliveries to a home address. This can be verified by checking with your Trucking Company's local agent. If shipment is to be made to your home and you live outside of town, also give your highway route number and some identifying landmarks. It is not necessary to send money to pay for truck transportation charges. You pay shipping charges to truck driver when goods are received.

HOW TO SEND MONEY

The best way to send money is by U. S. postal notes, by postoffice or express money order, or by bank draft or check. The mail carrier will be glad to buy a postoffice money order for you if you live on a rural route. It is better not to send coins, paper money or postage stamps with orders but should it be necessary, be sure to send your order by registered mail.

SEARS GUARANTEE

- To save you money
- To deliver all merchandise safely
- To satisfy you perfectly

We guarantee that every article in our catalogs is honestly described and illustrated. We guarantee that any article purchased from us will give you the service you have a right to expect. If for any reason whatever you are not satisfied with any article purchased from us, we want you to return it to us at our expense. We will then exchange it for exactly what you want, or will return your money, including any transportation charges you have paid.

SEARS, ROEBUCK AND CO.

In the 1970s, in another place, I became friends with the Wohlenburgs, who were both born in the 1890s. Mr. Wohlenburg, an educator who liked to pass on unusual facts, told me of a debate in Congress when it was proposed that first class postage be changed from two to three cents. Congressmen who argued against the proposal said they wanted to encourage people to communicate, and the higher postage may make it more difficult for some people. Postage remained at two cents. I wonder now if the three cents for sealed envelopes and two cents for tucked-flap envelopes may have been a compromise the next time the subject came up. I mailed envelopes both ways.

Packages, whether mailed by an individual or company, were wrapped in brown paper and tied with string. Individuals used brown paper from their grocery bags or bags in which other purchases were packaged. They also saved brown paper bags with which to line their cake pans if a certain cake needed a greased liner. There were no plastic shopping bags. Order string, as well as string from feed or flour sacks, was saved and used for packages and other string needs. Order string was the string which the depot agent used to attach orders to the Y rod for trainmen. Any type of box could be mailed, corrugated or not. If it was a new, unmarked box, paper wrapping wasn't necessary. Once in a while, a company would use brown packing tape. Individuals limited their use of tape; so paper could be reused—even on Christmas gifts. Adults of mid-twentieth century America had lived through the drought, the Great Depression, and World War II. They understood the adage, "Make it do or do without, use it up or wear it out." Not everyone practiced it; results of that became obvious in time. Mid-century America was wealthy compared to previous years of war, depression, and drought; but it was not affluent. That is, there were pockets and veins of affluence, but it had not saturated American society. Saturation wouldn't be long in coming.

Lamy had its own judge. He was Justice of the Peace, but we all called him Judge Salazar. His home was downhill from the curve by the Catholic Church. A person could reach his house by taking the second right hand turn coming into town; but, as children on our way to school or to a nearby home, we always ran down the hill and crossed directly in front of his house—between his house and the railroad track that heads to Santa Fe. It has been said that the Atlantic seaboard was settled by those who came for religious freedom, but that Spaniards who settled New Mexico came to be called Sir. Respect is a virtue of the old Spanish New Mexico. I have no idea what Judge Salazar's given name was; he was always Judge Salazar.

The Santa Fe Railroad's doctor was gone by the time I arrived. His office-home was the last home on the north fork of the road east of the depot. The McGuires bought his home from the Koepells and remodeled it. When they moved, they rented it a few months to Mr. and Mrs. Clarence Jewell (railroaders all), and then sold it to my parents. I was pleased to move near our friends, the Luceros and Heatherlys. We moved in on January 1, 1951, a cold morning.

C1952, The Doc Crume house, remodeled
Judy and Janelle Wootton and Madeline Archuleta
standing by their grandfather's car.

In the 1980s I corresponded with Dr. Crume's granddaughter who had been born in the doctor's office—my parents' bedroom. The best we could figure with my memory of the remodeled house and her memory of the original was that the original home was H-shaped. Facing the front of the house, the office was on the left (west) front side of the H, a bedroom at the front right (east) side of the H, living room and kitchen in the center and two bedrooms in the other ends of the H. She said the two back bedrooms had outside entrances and were rented to Lamy School teachers.

In the remodeled house the former kitchen became a utility room. The front right bedroom became the kitchen. The space between the two rear bedrooms was enclosed, making a den with knotty pine walls and ceiling, a stone fireplace, and red concrete floor. A small apartment was built onto the left rear bedroom.

On Mothers' Day 1967, an electrical fire destroyed the home. For years afterward, the fireplace stood, a lone mark of the Doc Crume house. The fireplace and the remains of the former chicken house are pictured on the next page.

Murder, Theft, and Fire

*L*amy had no jail; I guess it never did. In its early days, it attracted train robbers, gamblers, bunko men, and outlaws; but Lamy had tamed down decades before the mid-twentieth century arrived. Common human vices raised their head at times, as in any place people gather; but Lamy wasn't marked by crime.

There was one murder. Mr. ___, who lived between the mercantile store and the Gonzales' store, stabbed and killed Frank Gonzales with an ice pick. Mr. Gonzales died on January 1, 1955, and is buried in the Lamy Cemetery. The cemetery is less than a half mile back of the Catholic Church, an easy walk on a dirt road.

I remember Mr. Gonzales as a kind, gentle man. He had worked for the railroad and, as the father of several children, and had served several years on the Lamy School board in years gone by. His youngest son, Ralphie, and I started school together. The last time I saw Ralph, about 1966, he was a red cap at the A.T. & S.F. depot in Albuquerque. He had the same grin he always had. One night Mama heard sirens when she was visiting in the Santa Fe Railroad Hospital in Albuquerque. She said she found out later the sirens were for Ralph; someone killed him when he was a young man. Everything else seems small in light of that.

In my 1957 diary, I noted that my brother, a third grade student, told us someone broke into Lamy School the last week in September 1957. He didn't mention anything stolen or damage done.

The only theft I know of happened in the summer of 1953 at the Clayton's home next to the saloon. My brother and I played with their children, but they were family friends, as well. George and Edna Clayton were expecting their fourth child at any time; so Mrs. Clayton packed her suitcase and set it by the front door. One day, while they were in another room, someone knocked on the front door. The Claytons called, "Come in." The door opened and closed, but when they went into the living room, no one was there. Neither was the suitcase. The Claytons lived in Lamy a year or two while Mr. Clayton worked on a nearby ranch. They moved to Pecos, Texas, later that summer and gave us Mittens, their yellow tabby cat. I didn't know until years after her death that Mrs. Clayton had served as Texas' first elected female Sheriff (Sheriff, Tax Assessor-Collector, Loving County, Texas) before she moved to Lamy. Although another woman had served as an appointed sheriff many years before, Mrs. Edna Reed Clayton was the first woman elected sheriff in Texas. You'd never have guessed it to look at her.

Dad

One day, c1953, the Santa Fe county sheriff and a deputy knocked on our door. Someone matching Dad's description had robbed a loan company in Santa Fe; they were here to pick him up. Dad, went without resistance. All eighteen miles to Santa Fe the lawmen talked in Spanish, and Dad sat silently in the backseat. Meanwhile, at home, Mama was our stability. When dad and the officers arrived in Santa Fe, Dad stood in a line-up. No, the witness said, though he was tall and thin and wearing bib overalls, he was not the man.

The officers drove Dad back to Lamy. This time he joined their conversation. Surprised, they asked, "When did you learn Spanish?"

"I learned it from you on the way over," he answered.

Actually, he grew up in Cleveland, Mora, and Las Vegas, New Mexico, and spoke fluent Spanish.

My sister explained what had happened. When Dad got off work, he had taken his turn to pick up kids from school in Santa Fe and stopped at the gas station on Old Pecos Trail, where we regularly stopped for gas. He often traded guns and happened to have a rifle in the back window of his car.

Customers didn't pump their own gas in those days. An attendant came to the driver's window; the driver told him how much gas he wanted. The attendant put the gas in the tank and washed the car windows. As a result, one of the men at the station noticed the rifle when he serviced the car. He'd heard about the robbery and the description of the thief. He knew Dad's name, knew he was from Lamy, and reported him.

Fire was a more common problem—had been in the village's earlier years, still was. There was no fire department in Lamy. Being in Santa Fe County, the village depended on the Santa Fe fire department.

The first fire in mid-century Lamy was the Kirkendall home next to the Catholic Church. Stubs of the walls remained. It had been the home of railroader F. L. Kirkendall and his mother, whom the community called Grandma Kirkendall. I don't know if the Kirkendalls owned or rented the property. In 2018 the wall stubs appeared to have had some stabilization work done.

John, Janelle, and Judy Wootton at home, 1950, shortly before we watched the fire

The second house east of the agent's home was the next fire, in 1950. Adults hurried to help while waiting for the fire engine to arrive from Santa Fe. My sister was left in charge of my brother and me when our parents went to help. We watched the fire from our front porch, which later became the entrance to Frank's store. We could not see the house, but watched the orange red flames and haze transform into smoke against the dark night sky. The fire engine arrived too late; the house was demolished.

The third fire—c1952/53 started in the vacant storage building next to the general mercantile store. When the vacant building caught fire, the store and the attached saloon were saved. Whether there was much smoke damage or Mr. Brown, the storekeeper, used the opportunity to clear out old merchandise, I don't remember. I do know he had a smoke sale. Dad bought some new, old merchandise for which there had probably been no market since at least 1918: several pair of button shoes; a couple flat-cut, unadorned baby dresses, which he gave my sister and me for our dolls; and other items. Dad loved the past, not so much nostalgically, as wistfully wanting to include the past as part of the whole of life. He hit the jackpot at Mr. Brown's fire sale.

The last fire c1956/57 happened near the depot. A young couple had just purchased a brand new mobile home and had it parked where the diner had been located. They had it hooked up; but before they moved in, it caught fire—seems it had something to do with the electrical connection. The home wasn't demolished—it was open to walk through if a person wanted to look, but it wasn't liveable.

Housing

Unless a house was owned by the Santa Fe Railroad, individual families had to pay an annual lease to the property owner. Other than land owned by the Santa Fe Railroad and possibly the Catholic church, the village of Lamy was owned by an individual and sometimes changed hands. I questioned Mama about the lease when I was a small child. I'd seen her lower the drop leaf on her desk, get out her fountain pen, and write a check. A good one to dispel childhood fears, she explained that, though we owned our home, we had a 100-year land lease, which she paid every year. I figured it would be good at least until the turn of the century; so I didn't worry.

The Santa Fe Railroad built several houses and converted three boxcars into homes to make room for more families. With the exception of one boxcar home, all railroad homes were east of the depot. Though several railroaders lived west of the depot, they were more established in the area. They had come young and remained or were from established Lamy families. Every home in Lamy was within earshot of every passenger or freight train that came and went across the country—Chicago to Los Angeles and points between, day and night.

Besides the three converted boxcar houses, the Santa Fe had houses for the station agents, the track supervisor, and the signal maintainer; all were painted A.T. & S.F. yellow. Residents paid a minimal rent.

The railroad had also built a section house—the farthest east of all Lamy structures—as lodging for section crews; but it was deserted by mid-twentieth century. Winter, summer, spring, and fall wafted through the open doors and windows. Village children talked among themselves about the possibility of ghosts there, but were more concerned an actual hobo might be inside. To some children, hobos were the scariest possibility next to the booger man (bogeyman) or coco man, with whom some Lamy parents threatened their children if they didn't obey. I knew about the booger man from neighborhood children from the time I was two and assumed the coco man was similar. My parents maintained authority without the need of either. I never knew what the bogeyman looked like, but thought I saw him on Bridge Street in Las Vegas, New Mexico, when I was two and a half. A little more mature and more familiar with that area, I now think the bent, disheveled, dirty, little man walking down the street toward us was probably a wino. Who needed the threat of Santa's list of good and bad children when parents or older siblings could threaten one with the bogeyman or coco man?

There were hobos though they weren't frequently seen. In the early 1950s occasional transients or travelers who needed a place to stay until morning met Dad at the depot. He'd bring the man home. Mama would fold the burgundy-colored mohair sofa over into a bed and put on clean sheets. I suppose other families did the same. I know my maternal, non-railroad Grandfather did in Maxwell, New Mexico. One traveler made our home a regular stop if he needed a place to eat and sleep until he caught his train; railroaders called him "Thrill Kill." One day when Dad was driving the school carpool home from Santa Fe, we saw Thrill Kill on Old Pecos Trail. Dad instructed us to not look his way, but Thrill Kill waved us down. He climbed into the full car. There were no seat belts in those days; so everyone fit. He rode with us to Lamy, had supper and lodging, and went on his way the next day. We never had any trouble from our road-guests.

In addition to permanent housing, the Santa Fe Railroad also provided converted coach car homes on the rails; coach cars with their wheels could be moved from project to project, as needed. When in Lamy, they parked west of the depot—near the coal chute, across the road from the Catholic Church. When the Sanders family lived there, Mr. Sanders made a concrete wading pool for his girls. It added to the fun of our play that summer. With all her doilies, Mrs. Alva (Cleta) East made her coach car look like a doll house. Through my parents, I maintained contact with both families. As a child, I enjoyed my parents' friends. One time when I was in elementary school, Mama told me, "Go on now; I'm visiting with my friend." But from my teen years on, she shared Christmas letters and newspaper clippings pertaining to old friends, and told me news of them to help me keep in touch. In my adult years, I maintained personal friendships with Mrs. Sanders, Mr. East, and other mid-century Lamy residents.

Lamy had a community water system; some homes also had a well. Accustomed to the dry Southwest, those I knew well in Lamy enjoyed water wisely.

Electricity through a Santa Fe, New Mexico, source was available to all, but it was wise to have a kerosene lamp on hand for occasional power outages.

Betty Heatherly in the front yard of her railroad home.
The background shows the two railroad boxcars east of the depot.
John Wootton, Jr. added the little room seen on the one forefront.

Janice and Betty Heatherly in front of their railroad home c 1951.
Mr. Heatherly worked at the depot.

On the following page:

Janice Heatherly in the yard of her railroad home. The screened in porch of the station agent's home is on the left. The railroad mainline, not pictured, is to the right.

Next, a poor picture of Betty and Janice Heatherly shows their railroad home, which the Heatherlys had started remodeling. No one lived in the house after they moved, and the front yard soon filled with tree-of-Heaven trees. When I was four, I was so happy we were moving near our friends that I had to go tell Mr. Heatherly we were coming.

An outhouse, which belonged to one of the railroad's boxcar houses, 2018 photo

Most houses had indoor bathrooms; the boxcar houses and some others had outhouses.

Most homes had refrigeration although refrigerators had small freezer compartments. Washing was done in wringer washers or washtubs. Outer clothing was starched and then clothes were hung outside to dry. They dried quickly in the summer and freeze-dried in the winter, unless one wanted to string out a few things in the house.

Most homes were heated with wood/coal stoves or with kerosene oil. Before I started school, I rode to Madrid with Dad in the truck to get coal for our Warm Morning heater. Madrid, New Mexico, was an important coal supplier as long as the railroad used steam engines and homes used coal as their primary heat.

For cooking, homes had either wood/coal stoves or gas ranges, which used butane. A butane truck came to Lamy and filled butane tanks. Ours was in-ground near the fence line, where a cactus bloomed red in season and ants set up a hill. My friend and I dug up an ant hill once to see what it looked like underground. Very interesting, but we paid for the education. Mama put bluing on our bites.

Gardens and lawns were rare, but many homes had trees, bushes, vines, or flowers including peaches, apricots, grapes, pussy willow, honeysuckle, lilacs, tamarack, Virginia creeper, phlox, poppies, 4 o'clocks, hollyhocks, roses, gladiola, zinnia, and gourds. Green-tan, baseball size gourds grew in abundance along the railroad tracks. Lilacs were the most common and prolific of the household flowers. We took lilac bouquets to school.

The station agent's house was one of the few that had a lawn (on right). The picture shows one of the water storage tanks. I also have a picture of one on the south side of the road beyond the Doc Crume house—closer to the old section house; but, as in many pictures, structures were not the focus; so only a portion of that tank can be seen and is therefore not included.

Pictured in front of station agent Leo Zavilla's railroad home are his Pompeo grandchildren and their friends c1947, left to right: Paul Pompeo, Shirley Koons, Judy Wootton, Phyllis and Paula Pompeo.

Shirley is the daughter of railroader Gerald Koons and his wife, Alta.

Mr. Zavilla died in 1950. His wife, Marge, moved to Santa Fe to live with their daughter, Nora Pompeo and children. We visited them while we lived in Lamy. Mrs. Zavilla died in 1960; both Mr. and Mrs. Zavilla died in their 50s.

Mr. Zavilla worked for the railroad in Maxwell, New Mexico, before moving to Lamy. Eileen Wootton knew them when she lived with her brothers Bob and Henry Wilson and attended Maxwell High School.

Eileen's brother Bob and Nora's brother, Tedd, died while serving in the military during World War II. Bob went in on D-Day and died in the Battle of St. Lo, France, July 6, 1944. Tedd arrived in France in September 1944 and died during the advance on Breitenfeld. The battle was won, but his life was lost—two days after his birthday in April 1945.

Bob and Tedd were buried in Europe, but were returned to the United States after the War. In 1948, Bob was buried in the Wilson Cemetery on the Wilson Ranch, Chico Springs, Colfax County, New Mexico. In 1949, Tedd was buried in the Santa Fe National Cemetery in Santa Fe, New Mexico

If I knew the names of other losses that touched Lamy residents I would like to have paid tribute.

Faith and Religion

*E*very person has a belief system, but in mid-twentieth century America people, as a whole, connected beliefs with a church or religion. I don't mean to infer that everyone was religious or even attended church, but the majority of Lamy's residents were affiliated with the Catholic Church; and those who weren't Catholic were considered Protestants—at least in Lamy. Except for one family who lived in Lamy about a year, there were none who adhered to faiths termed cult or occult, nor were there any who followed Eastern religions.

A Catholic church had been built in Lamy in 1899, but a Mission Revival style church building with stained glass windows replaced it in 1926.

Our Lady of Light Catholic Church, late 1990s, photo courtesy of Jack McQuitty, Sr.

The new Our Lady of Light Catholic Church was built next to the road, as it curved to reveal the east end of Lamy when one entered Lamy or to reveal the west end of Lamy as one left. A priest, not a resident priest, held mass and advised his parishioners. There was an occasional funeral or wedding at the church. Eva Sanchez and Philip Chavez were married there on January 31, 1954, and had a reception at the bride's home before the evening dance at the Galisteo Dance Hall. Some couples, like Mr. and Mrs. Joe (Jose) Gonzales and Mr. and Mrs. Frank Gonzales, Jr. married in Santa Fe. Frank and his wife had their wedding dance at Tapia Hall in Lamy. Mr. and Mrs. Ralph Tapia had a large room, which was sometimes used for a party or a dance. Ladies also met at the Tapia's when they met for Red Cross for a short time.

Our Lady of Light Catholic Church, August 2018

In the late 1940s, Protestants didn't have a church building in Lamy, but met at Lamy School each Sunday morning. Though they came from different denominations, they worshipped together. Reverend Bulkeley rode the Indian Detours bus from Santa Fe every Sunday morning and preached at the school house church after the Sunday School hour. He was a tall, older man of medium build and wore suspenders. Members of the congregation took turns inviting Rev. Bulkeley to dinner in their home after the service. He then walked to the depot and rode the next Indian Detours bus back to Santa Fe.

Below is a bulletin from the church that met at Lamy School.
On the next page is a Cradle Roll Certificate from the Lamy Sunday School.

Our Sunday School.

Lamy, New Mexico, Sunday, June 30, 1946

(Matt. 16:18) And I say also unto thee, That thou art Peter, and upon this rock I will build my church; and the gates of hell shall not prevail against it.

At our first meeting, Sunday, June 16, 1946, we had a total attendance of 36 for Sunday School and 38 for church.

At our second meeting, Sunday, June 23, we had a total attendance of 20 in Sunday School and 20 in church.

As we enter into the third and fourth weeks, we must make every possible effort to enlarge and increase our attendance. Our present goal is to have an enrollment of 50 and an average attendance of 40. We can and will attain this goal if each of us, individually, will bring our wives, husbands, relatives, friends, and neighbors.

The Home Mission Board of the Baptist Church has offered to help us with a Daily Vacation Bible School. They will furnish the necessary literature and two teachers for a full two week course. If we wish to do this it will be necessary for us to keep the two teachers for the two weeks they will be here. I would like to hear from everyone as to whether or not this is favorable to you. Would also like to know if any of you can keep one or both of the teachers.

Birthday Greetings:
Mrs. J. P. Wootton, who reached the age of ?? on June 1, 1946.
Mrs. W. R. Mallory who is now ?? years of age as of June 14, 1946.
Mrs. Robert Cooper, who will be ?? on July 1, 1946.
Robert Cooper, who will be one year older than Mrs. Cooper on July 1, 1946.
Mrs. P. H. Burgeis will be one year older than here present age after July 4, 1946.

If each class will select a correspondent we will carry reports of each class every Sunday.

CRADLE ROLL
CERTIFICATE

This Certifies that *Janell Wootton*

born on _____ day of _____ 19___ has been

enrolled as a member of the CRADLE ROLL DEPARTMENT of

the *Larry Sundy* school

this ___26th___ day of _____ 19___

Mrs. Raymond Malloy.
SUPT. CRADLE ROLL

Mrs. Robert Belcher,
SUPT. SCHOOL

S. L. Bulkeley
MINISTER

The community church had disbanded by the time school started in 1949; so those who were not Catholic and wanted to attend church drove in to Santa Fe or, on rare occasion, rode the Indian Detours bus.

Ready to leave for church in Santa Fe, May 1958
Back: Janelle and Judy Wootton
Front: Mary Jane Taylor, John Wootton III, and Myles Lark

In the 1950s, from c1951-mid 1955, Bible studies were held in homes. They were in the Wootton home at first, but the Harwells and Lehmans hosted the meetings on occasion. One evening each week, Pastor Robert Brown and his wife drove out from Santa Fe to lead in the chapter-by-chapter Bible study. Often the children sat on chairs or on the floor and listened; but sometimes Mrs. Brown taught them separately. The group sang, using small, spiral bound songbooks prepared for the Billy Graham Crusade in Albuquerque and sold afterward. Bible study followed, ending with a time of refreshments and visiting. Those who attended the studies either attended church in Santa Fe or were unchurched. One of my favorite refreshments was Mama's almond wedding cookies rolled in powdered sugar. I enjoyed the entire meeting from the singing to the fellowship. I didn't mind the times we had to sit on the floor and never remember being bored with the lessons.

Not long after the studies began, one little girl at Lamy School told Judy Wootton that the priest had told the children not to play with her because the Woottons had Bible classes in their home; but, the little girl said, she was going to play with her anyway; and she did. When the class played baseball, there were two teams: Judy and Rosa on one team and the rest of students on the other.

Before their younger daughter started school, one longtime family friend moved for their girls to attend school elsewhere. Our friend, the mother, told me years later that in the mid-1940s children received Catholic instruction before school. Students who didn't participate in Catholic instruction—including her oldest child—had to wait outside until instruction was done, regardless of the weather.

There was no Catholic instruction by the time my siblings and I attended school in Lamy. Neither did I experience alienation, but then the lady who was the teacher when I started, would not have allowed it even though I understood she was Catholic.

Mama, Mrs. Wootton, taught a weekly Good News Club in our home from 1954 through the end of 1958. Children sang, listened to visualized missionary stories and flannelgraph Bible stories, and memorized Bible verses. There were incentive games and prizes. Mama grew up without parties of her own and knew that many other children did, also; so during the years she taught Good News Club, she had holiday parties for all the children who came. The party belonged to all of them. Her desserts varied, but she had a staple punch, which she made of orange juice and Kool-Aid. For a short time when I was eleven and my friend Mary Jane Taylor was eight, she and I had a similar class for little girls on Saturdays.

Our Saturday group, January or February 1958
Back: Dolores and Carol Samaniego, Mary Jane Taylor
Front: Charlotte and Myra Carbajal

Life in Lamy

*M*id-twentieth-century American life was post-war life. Was there a neighborhood or a family that was not represented in the nation's World War II effort? Who did not have a family member, friend, or neighbor who had not been injured or killed? Though it was a small village, Lamy, New Mexico, was no different.

Lamy had reached its census peak by 1940. By the time the drought and depression of the 1930s and the war of the early 1940s were over, the population had been reduced. A couple of times when my sister and I would lie awake at bedtime in the mid-1950s and count the population of the village, we counted 125. At that time, we knew the names of everyone in every house in Lamy. The village population had been twice that in 1900 and was well over 300 in 1930 and 1940. I don't know the official population in 1950. If there were street names, we never heard tell of anyone who knew them though we called the road that led to the Dr. Crume house, Nob Hill.

Lamy was close enough to Santa Fe and Albuquerque and small enough in itself that no newspaper was needed. One Christmas I received a Hectograph. A Hectograph had a gelatinous surface about the size of an 8.5" x 11" sheet of paper. With an indelible pencil, copy was written on a sheet of paper and transferred to the surface of the Hectograph. One-by-one sheets of paper could be placed on the Hectograph so that the print would transfer. My friend Mary Jane and I used it to publish a one page newsletter-type, weekly newspaper for one or two weeks.

Mary Jane and I also did Magic Shows one summer. Comic books had deals in the back, and we allowed ourselves to be taken in by a comic book ad. We pooled our resources—twenty-five cents each—and ordered a magic book. Once we had the paper booklet in hand, we realized our mistake. In order to recoup our losses, we set up chairs in our front yard under the apricot tree and held magic shows. Between our siblings and our mothers, the entry fees soon covered our losses; and we went out of business.

Lamy was a blue collar community. Most men worked for the Santa Fe Railroad; some worked in construction or on nearby ranches or in the local store or saloon. Few women worked outside the home.

Women cooked from scratch, baked any deserts they served their family; many made tortillas or fresh bread regularly. They washed and hung clothes to dry on a clothesline, gathered them in, and sprinkled down any that needed ironed. They ironed dresses, blouses and skirts, aprons, shirts and pants, and dresser scarves. Some ironed bed linens. They sewed, mended, and patched clothes to make them

last. They cleaned — swept, mopped and waxed floors, dusted, washed windows and walls. They cared for the children and taught them skills. The amount and kind varied, but most children also had chores to do. Carmen, a nine-year-old friend whose mother worked at the depot, cooked beans and tortillas for the family's lunch everyday. Carmen, at age 6, is pictured on the left, leaving for school with Judy Wootton in the Fall of 1951. Carmen was a loyal friend from preschool days until she died in Georgia in June 2015.

For those who used wood or coal heat in any manner, there was wood to chop or coal to carry in, fires to be kept, ashes to be taken out. Life was more hands-on, work-intensive without instant or quick-prep foods and with fabrics that required more care with the era's high standards of neatness. Few had many labor saving appliances and devices.

School age children all played together at school; but after school or during the summer, they played with children closest to their homes. Once in a while, a child would walk a distance to see a friend, but it wasn't handy for regular play.

Neighborhood children standing on the road in front of the depot c1951:
Back: Ricky Lucero, Judy Wootton, Betty and Janice Heatherly
Front: John III and Janelle Wootton and Carmen Lucero
The diner can be seen at the right.

Friends on the road in front of the Lamy depot c1950, left to right:
Janice Heatherly, Judy Wootton, Betty Heatherly, Janelle Wootton

Because walking, except for special occasions, was the mode of transportation, women also tended to visit with women who lived nearby. In the mid-late 1940s a group of ladies, who called themselves the Ladies' Sewing Circle or Homemakers' Club, met weekly in homes east of the depot. The ladies took turns hosting the group in their homes. They brought their mending or handwork and visited and had refreshments as they worked. Their children came along and played together.

Ladies' Sewing Circle 1947: Margaret Sanders, Christine Belcher, Alta Koons, Mrs. Montgomery's daughter, Mrs. Montgomery, Marge Zavilla with Janelle Wootton, Eileen Wootton, Violet Mallory and _____ with her baby son.

Summers were a nice time for mothers to take their children to play or have a picnic on the railroad lawn, next to the depot—where the El Ortiz was once located. Children who lived near the school could enjoy playing in the schoolyard.

Children had toys, but few toys. They enjoyed imaginative/pretend play. Soldiers and army were big during and after the war; cowboys and cowgirls captured the stage in the 1950s. A broom could serve as a horse as well as any store-bought stick horse. If the cowboy or soldier had no weapon, a stick would do. Girls enjoyed playing house or school, doll furniture, and paper dolls. Paper dolls—or extra clothing for store-bought paper dolls—were sometimes cut out of an old catalog. Though skating was popular in some places, there weren't enough sidewalks in Lamy to learn to skate with proficiency. Some rode tricycles or bicycles.

Tree climbing was fun and free. Mrs. Crume had been thoughtful enough to plant trees in our yard so that they were climbing size by the time we got there. Some children had swings; ours was a tree swing. Carmen and Rickie Lucero, who lived in the agent's house, had a real swing set. Carmen once swung over the top.

Myles Lark, Donnie Samaniego, John Wootton

Outside of our yard we found clay dirt on a little rise near the road. When we wanted to play bakery, we made more permanent baked goods out of clay, rather than our usual mud desserts.

When it snowed, children enjoyed playing in the snow, sledding, having snowball fights, and making snowmen.

Few had birthday parties. Party gifts were simple, like a coloring book, a handkerchief, or a barrette. Refreshments were cake and Kool-Aid, sometimes served with whipped Jell-O or ice cream. Pin-the-tail-on-the-Donkey, Musical Chairs and Musical Shoe, Gossip, and I'm Going on a Trip were some favorite birthday games.

Back: Esther Muller, Cecilia Gonzales, Judy Wootton, Betty Heatherly
Front: Janelle Wootton, Betty Salazar, Janice Heatherly, ___, and Rosa
Chavez. Birthday party, 1950, at the house across from the depot

Back: Ricky Lucero, Judy Wootton, Carmen Lucero
Front: Jimmy and Willie Turner, John and Janelle Wootton, Donnie
Chandler, Speck. Turners were children of signal maintainer Jess Turner.
Back building is the apartment on the remodeled Doc Crume house.

Besides birthdays and Christmas, children also enjoyed Halloween and May Day. For Halloween trick-or-treating, some children had store-bought masks. Our family had three rubber masks to choose from year after year: a wolf; a long-nosed, bald man; and a face with cuts and stitches. Usually, with the help of parents or older siblings, we children used what we had to dress as a ghost, pirate, cowboy, or gypsy. It was cold in Lamy on Halloween; so most of one's costume would be covered by a coat, anyway. The only warmth on Halloween night was inside a rubber mask where it was so warm that the cold night air met one's warm breath and liquefied.

Halloween treats were simple—an apple or graham cracker, a cookie, a piece of fudge or a popcorn ball, a piece of taffy, a sucker. Not all candy was wrapped, even at the store. Once in a while, some trick-or-treater would write on a window with a piece of wax. If a Jack-o-lantern was carved, it would be cooked and used afterward. We enjoyed buying flavored, shaped wax, which was available only at Halloween; there were red wax lips and black wax moustaches. More fun, but twice the price was an orange wax whistle, which had several holes to blow through in order to make music; but one by one, we'd eat off the length of each hole, each time lessening our ability to make music. We chewed that wax a long time, like gum.

Halloween was receiving; May Day was giving. We were told that in some parts of the United States children gave baskets of flowers on May 1st. That was a little early for flowers in Lamy; so mothers made edible goodies, usually a combination of cookies and candies, to be put in baskets. Ahead of time, families saved containers that could be made into baskets. Strawberry baskets were ideal, but they were rare. Washed tin cans worked. Children covered and decorated them and added a little handle. On the morning of May 1st, before children left for school or church, they packed baskets with goodies and delivered them to neighbors' homes. They set the basket on the doorstep, knocked on the door, and ran lickety-scoot to hide before anyone answered the door and saw who left the basket. Once the neighbor went back into the house and closed the door, the children left to deliver the next basket. They couldn't deliver to everyone because of the time element; so they delivered to those who lived near. Some left baskets at our house. We usually didn't know who left the basket; however, we recognized one by the taste of the mother's fudge. We especially enjoyed leaving a basket for Mr. and Mrs. (Nettie) Walter Mallory, a retired railroader and his wife, who were so kind at Halloween. Her mother, Mrs. Sandlin, lived with them.

Walter Mallory in his yard, c1957

Lamy was on Mountain Standard Time year round. That gave neighborhood children time to play games that are better in the dark—games like hide-n-go-seek, sardines, run sheep run, and kick the can. In daylight, they played group games like tag, freeze tag, sling the statue, sword tag, school on the stairs, Red Rover, and London Bridges. At times, in late afternoon or on non-school days, children in our neighborhood gathered on the dirt road and played softball. There was little traffic.

Teams were chosen and then the bat was tossed in the air by the two captains. They placed fist over fist until one hand reached the top of the bat. That leader's team batted first. There were two drawbacks to playing on the road in front of our house: Rover and a short stretch where the sewer ran open between piped areas. Once in a while, Dad thought it would be fun for Rover to be off of his chain; and what more fun could there be for him than to join a ball game? We hated when Rover caught the ball; but the slobbery ball was one notch above having to retrieve a ball out of the sewer.

At one time there had been a men's baseball team in Lamy. The team didn't exist in the 1950s, but one could still see their ball field west of Lamy School. I noticed it when I was a child and asked Mama about it.

Many established Lamy families had relatives in the village. Young railroad families in the late 1940s did not; therefore, many of them formed friendships that lasted a lifetime. The men worked long and hard; but, if they got off in time, the young families sometimes picnicked together on a summer evening. Men played ball, women visited, and children played. I was a baby; so I got hung in a swing on a tree limb. When Mama told me about it, I believe she worded it differently.

During World War II, many ordinary take-it-for-granted items had been rationed or were scarce—from ordinary things like meat and sugar to tires and vehicles. After the war, some needs escalated because of people returning from military service to establish or reestablish homes. It was a while after the war before my parents owned a washing machine. Alta Koons, whose husband was also a railroader, invited Mama to come do laundry at her house. Alta and Mama did their wash together while their girls played, and then fixed lunch and ate together.

If Mama wanted to shop in Santa Fe while Dad was at work, she could ride the Indian Detours bus; but she sometimes rode to town with Mrs. Boyce or another neighbor. When it was time for me to be born, Mrs. Boyce drove Mama to the hospital. Mama didn't get her driver's license until years later; but once she did, she used her car for others as long as she drove.

When Conductor John Casick and his wife Ellen wanted to move their eight-foot-wide mobile home to Lamy in 1950, our family drove to Albuquerque to help. Mama and we kids rode home with Mrs. Casick in their car. From time-to-time I'd look back and watch Dad and Mr. Casick pulling the mobile home with our truck. They parked the trailer at the fork of the road east of the depot. The little house had a restroom and a place to wash, but it didn't have a shower. Casick told me they went into Santa Fe once a week and rented a motel room; so they could shower. Later an addition was built onto the mobile home.

People worked long and hard and were grateful for time to visit. They made time to visit. People didn't call to say, I'm coming over. They went. Sunday afternoons were an especially nice time to walk over and visit a neighbor or to exchange visits with out-of-town relatives. Sometimes people wrote to invite out-of-town friends or family for a visit or to say they were going to visit; sometimes they just went. One time we left to visit out-of-town relatives. We passed each other on the highway, but saw each other. They turned around and we all went to their house.

The Woottons with visitors from Las Vegas, New Mexico, c1950.
House in the background is across from the depot.
Back: Clarence and Pauline Chandler, Judy, Eileen and Joe Wootton, Madeline
Archuleta. Front: Donnie Chandler, Bobbie Joe Archuleta, Janelle Wootton

People—family and friends—didn't always agree; so? There were pouty people here and there. Some would hold onto an offence; but, for the most part, friends in those days were solid, not petty, nor impetuous. To be honest, I must admit friendship could be bought on rare occasions. When I was 3½, John Casick bought me a bag of candy all my own and made a friend for life. Of course, his personality helped. His wife, Ellen, bought a bag for my sister.

Years later I visited with another railroader, about fifteen years Casick's junior. He said Casick talked big about himself. The man failed to notice that Casick talked big about everyone. I never considered him an egotist. Rather, I saw John Casick as one who saw the good in others and in life and spoke it, whether it was about himself or another. He enjoyed conversation, had a ready smile and a friendly laugh. It never seemed an inconvenient time for him to take time for a friend or to make a new one. Ellen and he had no children. She died first—in

1986; he made it into the 21st century. He died at the Miners' Hospital in Raton, New Mexico, in May 2010. Both are buried in Embudo, New Mexico.

Lamy was close to good fishing spots in the Pecos, New Mexico, area; so those who enjoyed fishing didn't have far to go. On our way to Pecos we liked to stop at the store in Rowe, especially if Dad bought a long, thin, circular-shaped tube of bologna. He thought the slices tasted good on saltine crackers; we did, too. Mama always packed tasty lunches, but the bologna and crackers were a nice addition. Dad kept a canvas water-bag filled with water. It hung on the hood ornament as we traveled down the road, in case any of us or the vehicle needed water. Once we were at the river, we had all the water we wanted right from the stream.

Some of Dad's favorite fishing spots were Cowles' Creek, the Beaver Dams, and the Pecos River near the Benedictine Monastery and near the fish hatchery. We children liked to see the varied sizes of fish at the hatchery and admired the shiny silver, copper, and nickel coins at the bottom of the tank where the largest fish swam. We enjoyed building sand castles or gathering sticks and mud to make farms or ranches. We waded in the river. Mama taught us to wade with a walking stick because one never knows the holes or depths of a stream. Except for the Sanders' little wading pool, there was nothing like wading or swimming in or near Lamy. We knew we were to be decent about our play and not be noisy, or we'd scare the fish. Usually Dad put on his waders, carried his creel, and walked up or down stream from us. Mama took embroidery work or reading for her relaxation.

On occasion, neighbor children went fishing with us. When we took the truck, we children sat in the back of the truck near the cab; Dad never let us sit near the tailgate. Sitting in the truck bed, we sang songs with several verses, like "Found a Peanut," or songs in rounds, like "Row, Row, Row Your Boat." Except for one time, we invited those who went with us. We had a good friend—she really was, but Marsha had a way about her. Those of us bred and taught in the old New Mexico culture wouldn't think of inviting ourselves. In fact, in some instances, we would have to be asked more than once, just in case the first invitation was out of politeness; but Marsha always included herself. One day when we went fishing at the Beaver Dams, she invited herself. She had no fishing pole, but found a stick and some string and came along. An avid fisherman, Dad wasn't too pleased; but his New Mexico manners held him in check. Marsha hopped in the truck, enjoyed the ride. She didn't even seem bothered like I was when nettles stuck in our socks as we walked across the field to the fishing spot. She got a hook and bait from Dad—and out-fished him. Dad took it good-naturedly; the rest of us grinned, and we all retold the story. Marsha and her family moved from Lamy in 1955. Poor thing, she had asthma and died during an attack in Raton in her early adult years.

Lamy had good radio reception from Santa Fe and Albuquerque. On stormy winter mornings reception would be a bit crackly; but Mama always kept abreast of news and weather, especially as it might affect our school day. When I was preschool, I liked to sit on the floor next to speaker on the radio-phonograph and listen to popular music and old style country-western music on Albuquerque's KOB station. Even then I enjoyed writing; so I penciled in a triangle on one of the little squares of the speaker's cloth covering. I thought nothing more of it until I mentioned it to Mama fifty years later. She said she'd wondered about that. It was a good time for me to confess. Now that the phonograph no longer worked, it didn't matter.

My parents purchased a television when I was seven. Neighborhood children enjoyed watching with us; but we had too much playing to do once our chores were done to give television all our free time. Because of its proximity to Albuquerque, which had three television stations, Lamy had good reception while larger communities to the north had snowy reception for years. Everyone who had a television had an outdoor antenna, which reached into the sky above their home. Lamy received all three Albuquerque stations: KOB-4, KGGM-13, and KOAT-7. Sometimes KOAT pictures had a snowy quality. Stations shut down programming during the night and began with a test pattern in the morning. Perhaps the test pattern was on all the time the station was off the air; I don't know.

Lamy had better public transportation than most towns and some cities do in the early twenty-first-century. Three cross-country passenger trains and one combination freight-passenger train ran east, and the same number ran west everyday; each stopped in Lamy. If you couldn't reach your destination on the mainline, there were other trains that connected passengers to further destinations on the coasts and in the heartland of America. If a person didn't want to travel by rail, he could board one of the Indian Detours buses that met each passenger train in Lamy, travel to Santa Fe, and board a Greyhound bus. The Greyhound depot was within easy walking distance of the Indian Detours depot.

When I was five, my mother and I went to Santa Fe on the bus and walked to the Greyhound depot, where she helped me board a bus to go visit my Aunt Mary Martin who lived 145 miles away. Perhaps my parents thought it was safer for a child to travel alone on a bus, seated behind the driver, than to travel alone on the train—or perhaps it was because Aunt Mary had a Greyhound office in her mom and pop store and knew the bus drivers. I never asked. I sat in the seat behind the driver and visited with a nice lady and looked at the scenery. We stopped at towns and villages all along the way.

Life in Lamy Album

Central Lamy, New Mexico, as the road curves past
Our Lady of Light Catholic Church toward the depot
Photo by Jack McQuitty, Sr., late 1990s
Used by permission

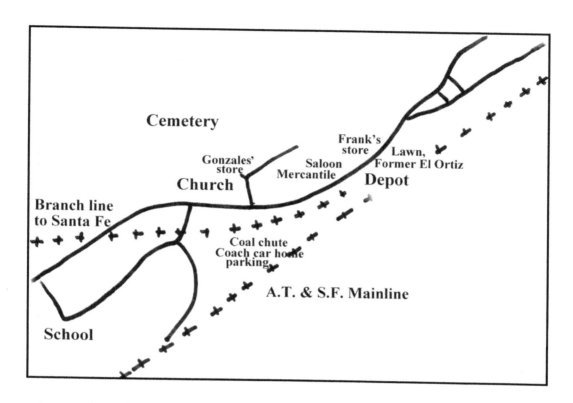

An overview of mid-twentieth century Lamy, not to scale. Solid lines represent roads. Lines of spaced pluses represent railroad tracks; these serve only to note location of tracks. The mainline in Lamy was not a single set of tracks.
The place where coach car homes parked is noted.
Some who lived in coach car homes: Sanders, East, Smith

The mercantile store and Frank's store did not operate simultaneously. After Frank's store opened, the mercantile and saloon areas combined into the Pink Garter Saloon. Many years later it became The Legal Tender.

The following pages divide this map into three sections, with numbers representing structures. They are the ones I remember; I may have left out a couple. I have included the names of families I know who lived in the house numbered, as well as the names of those I have heard of who lived there.

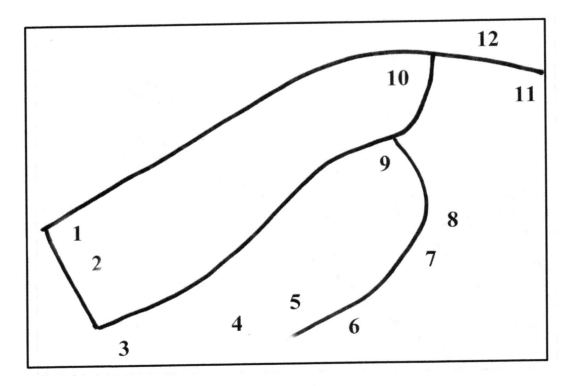

1. Carrillo/Carillo: Eddie, a student at Lamy school, his grandma, and his uncle Juan
2. Irene
3. Lamy School
4. Sena. My sister said her friends Corine and Frances lived there.
5. Sanchez. Mariquita Sanchez's family home. She was a sister of Mrs. Cordova.
6. Cordova family. My sister, brother, and I went to school with the Cordova children.
7. Mr. and Mrs. Tapia, Tapia Hall
8. Vigil. Their son Ray rode to Santa Fe school with us in the Fall of 1958.
9. Anaya, Chavez. Two of my good friends lived there: Julia Anaya and Millie Chavez.
10. This was a railroad boxcar home. Jones, Howell, Koons
11. Judge Salazar's house. He, his wife, and their granddaughter Betty lived there.
12. Kirkendall house, which burnt down.

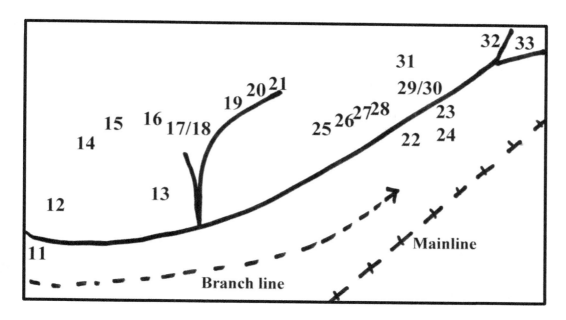

11. and 12. Noted on previous map

13. Our Lady of Light Catholic Church

14. and 15. Homes of the Mares and Montoya families. I'm not sure which was which.

16. Gonzales home and store

17. Quatro Muller family. 17 and 18 was a large duplex-type, gray stucco house. I only remember the Mullers in 17. I heard his name was Eusebio, but we knew him as Quatro.

18. Colvet, Sandy

19. Griego

20. and 21. I think there may have been one more house up on the ridge with 19-21. I do not have straight who lived where, but a Chavez family and a Gonzales family lived in the houses. Whether with the Chavezes or alone, there was a Chavez Grandma and aunt. I think the Sandy family also lived in one of these houses for a short time.

22. Santa Fe Railroad Depot

23. Diner. Then vacant until a new mobile home was parked there, burnt

24. Former site of El Ortiz. In mid-century this was a large lawn, owned by A.T. & S.F.

25. Vacant building used as storage in the early 1950s

26. Mercantile store and post office

27. Saloon

28. Clayton

29. Wootton

30. Villanueva. Later 29 and 30 became the combined Villanueva store and home.

31. There may have been two houses here. Mr. Brown; Mr. and Mrs. Blea with their 3 legged dog. I never saw Mrs. Blea without a cleaning-type scarf wrapped on her head.

32. Koons, Howell, Scarbrough, Sandy

33. Casick, Shearmire

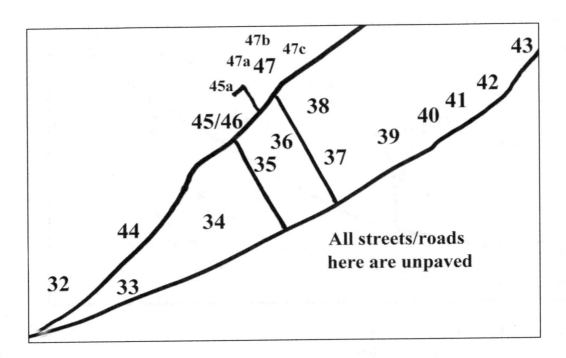

32 and 33 on previous page

34. Ingraham, Bonney

35/36 Boxcar houses. 35.: Boyce, various families and single railroaders. Of all the houses in Lamy, people seemed to move in and out of this one the most.

36. Wootton, Carbajal

37. Montgomery, Heatherly

38. McBroom. After Heatherlys moved, McBrooms had a mobile home here a short time.

39. Zavilla and Pompeo (Zavilla's daughter and children), Lucero

40. Sanchez; Loraine Sanchez lived here with her grandparents. Related to Bleas. Sometimes the 3-legged dog was with Loraine.

41. Cooper, Blea; house burnt, 1950.

42. Walter and Nettie Mallory and her mother, Mrs. Sandlin

43. Koons, Jewell, McGinnis

44. For a short time Jim and Angie Muller Sandy lived here in a mobile home.

45/46 was a large clapboard railroad house, painted Santa Fe Railroad yellow:

45. Creed (pre-mid-century), East, Turner, Harwell, Mahannah (also, Lark, Taylor, children). 45b. Signal maintainer's garage

46. Bob Mallory family, Lehman (also her children Marsha and Tom Everett), Samaniego

47. Crume, Koepell, McGuire, Jewell, Wootton; 47b: chicken house; 47c: garages, storage shed

47a. Apartment: Pitt, Goforth, Albin, Green, Jenkins, Rumley

Not listed: A.T. & S.F. section house, around the curve past number 43.

Lamy, New Mexico, 1958

©Janelle Wootton

Fall 1958. When I knew I must leave Lamy, I climbed a hill behind the Doc Crume house and took this picture. My camera scope was limited; so only a portion of the village is seen. It does show the Doc Crume house forefront, to its right the railroad duplex house, also two boxcar houses, as well as the depot with an Indian Detours bus parked in front. A portion of Lamy Mountain is on the right.

Sandy, Margaret, and Carol Sanders c1947

Johnnie and Eileen Wootton with daughters, Judy and Janelle, in the yard of their boxcar home. Behind them is a garage that belonged with that home.

Paul Pompeo, Judy Wootton, and Phyllis Pompeo, c1947/48

Mrs. Boyce with her grandson, c1948. About this time, Mrs. Boyce received a new coat. Many of the era, having been through World War II and the depression, saved the new and used the old. Mrs. Boyce wore her new coat, saying, "Who knows? I may die and my husband's new wife would get to wear it." She died within a few years. It's a good thing she enjoyed her coat.

Back:
Judy Wootton,
Carol Sanders,
Eileen Wootton,
Sandy Sanders
Front: Janelle
and John
Wootton

In the
background the
Ingraham -
Bonney house
and one of the
boxcar houses.

View from the road in front of the depot, Spring 1950. The fork in the road and houses numbered 34 and 35 on the map can be seen because the photo was taken shortly before John and Ellen Casick brought their trailer from Albuquerque and parked it at the fork. The structure to the left is a shed belonging to the house which later became Frank Villanueva's store. Janelle Wootton faces the depot.

David and Susan Albin, children of Alan and Amelia Albin. Late 1955/early 1956.
Amelia and her brother, railroader Manuel Bonney, who lived nearby, were related
to Billy the Kid's Bonney family. Children are seated on the porch of the apartment
the callboy entered when running from Rover. Susan died August 3, 1956.

Neighbors John Wootton and Christine Mahannah celebrate their mutual birthdays. Christine's husband, Earl, was signal maintainer at the time, 1958.

Mary Jane Taylor, daughter of Christine Mahannah, 1957. There is clay dirt on the side of the embankment just down from the pile of rocks, upper right.

Education

*L*amy education had its high and low points. I was blessed to attend Lamy School during good years. With a growing population, the community had built a school in 1929.

Lamy School was the first structure to greet people as they entered mid-twentieth century Lamy by the highway. By rail, Lamy School was the furthermost west and the abandoned railroad section house the furthermost east; so, depending on which way one came by rail, it was the first or the last. Its playground bordered the railroad tracks.

A fine Pueblo style building, the 4,341 square foot school had four classrooms, two restrooms, a principal's office, and a window-walled, long, wide front corridor, which led to each of the other rooms. Outside there was a door to the cellar where coal was kept to heat the school. It was heated not with a furnace, but with a large wood-coal stove in the classroom.

The 5.782 acre plot on which the school was built gave children plenty of room for imaginative play. The building was close to the front of the lot. In the back playground area were three pieces of play equipment, each built of the study wood of bygone years: a two or three-teeter-totter unit, a swing set, and a merry-go-round. During the 1954-55 school year, a jungle gym/monkey bars was added on the west side of the front playground. Girls were required to wear shorts or pants under their dresses if they played on the monkey bars.

All grades played together at recess, generally boys with boys and girls with girls. Sometimes they played together—as when they played war. The boys played soldiers gone off to war; they went way down the long rectangular school lot, while the girls maintained the home front on the merry-go-round. They waited as nurses to care for the wounded. Children played unsupervised—as far as they knew—because the teacher, who taught more than one grade had plenty of work to do. Of course, the teacher may have seen more than students realized because three of the classrooms had windows across the side that faced the back playground.

114

There was no organized physical education program, but there were times all of the students played supervised games together, games like "The Mole," "A Tisket, a Tasket, a Red and Yellow Basket" and "Bluebird." There were other little playground games they played by themselves, like Colors and London Bridges. When my sister was at Lamy School, they also played baseball.

The school may have originally taught grades one through nine or twelve. Even in the 1950s some schools had a graduation ceremony for those who completed the ninth grade. For some students that was the end of their education.

Anita Samaniego, daughter of track supervisor Raymond Samaniego, on the day she graduated from ninth grade, Leah Harvey Jr. High, Santa Fe, May 1958. The background shows the drive way to the homes of the track supervisor and the signal maintainer.

Although there were four classrooms in Lamy School, only two were used as classrooms by 1949. That year, 1949-50, Mrs. Herrera from Santa Fe taught pre-first-second grade. My sister was in her second grade class. Mrs. DeZeke from Las Vegas, New Mexico, taught third through sixth grades in the other room. I'm not sure if that is how she spelled her name, but that is how it sounded.

Mrs. Herrera didn't miss school; but she often fell asleep in class. When there were visitors from the county school department, she kept her eyes wide open and on the students in such a manner they knew they better toe the mark.

Mrs. Herrera had noticed that not all older students knew the days of the week and the months of the year. She made certain that her students learned them; that was her strong emphasis.

The next year, 1950-51, Mr. Gonzales taught the upper grade classroom. A good teacher, his was the last Lamy class to include fifth and sixth grades.

In 1951-52, classes through fourth grade were taught in one classroom with Mrs. Herrera as teacher. When Mrs. Herrera needed to be out of the room for awhile, she'd appoint fourth graders to take charge of one grade each. There were just enough fourth graders to go around; the older students enjoyed being in charge. This wasn't something done only at Lamy School. In Santa Fe, my second grade classroom was next to the principal's office because my teacher, Mrs. Verna Walker, was assistant principal. When the principal, Mr. John Russell, was gone, Mrs. Walker was sometimes needed in the office. While she was gone, one or two sixth graders were called to come downstairs and take charge of her class.

On occasion Lamy School had trouble keeping the same teacher throughout the school year or finding teachers who had a good command of English. That was more of a problem when my sister attended Lamy School. I encountered neither problem. However, I was led to believe I may have had a different opinion of Lamy School if I had not attended second grade in Santa Fe; I have no knowledge of the school or teacher that year.

Red-headed Mariquita Sanchez, the janitor, was a constant through the years my sister, brother, and I attended Lamy School. Though teachers came and went, Mariquita remained, keeping the classroom clean and comfortable. In cold weather she went to school early and started the fire in the classroom's large wood/coal stove; so the room would be warm and comfortable by the time class started.

For the students' Christmas program c1950 or 1951, Mariquita doubled as Santa Claus, handing out treats. A thin lady, Mariquita had a hard time trying to keep her pillow-stomach from slipping. My mother, brother, and I went to watch my sister in the Christmas program. Mama was surprised none of the children noticed Mariquita's slipping stomach, but everyone was too glad to see Santa and to receive candy to pay attention to Santa's problem.

Mariquita had a gold tooth. I'd lost a tooth shortly before Mama and I visited in her home. Mariquita told me if I didn't put my tongue in the place of the missing tooth, I'd get a gold tooth like hers. From then on, every time I lost a tooth I tried to keep my tongue out of the tooth-hole. I now have two gold teeth—but not because of any success controlling my tongue.

On the following pages are pictures taken by Eileen Wootton.

Lamy School 1949-50
I don't know if any of the students are absent.
My sister, Judy Wootton Mendez, helped identify some of these.

Picture 1, Grades Pre-first-2
Back: Mrs. Herrera, teacher
Center: Jesusita Cordova and her sister Lupe Cordova, Rosa Chavez, Judy Wootton, Susie Jones, Janice Heatherly
Front: Rudolfo Montoya, Mary Lou Gonzales, Betty Salazar, Lalo Cordova, ___ , Leo Montoya, Isidro Muller

Picture 2, Grades 3-6
Back: Lupe Chavez, Eva Sanchez, Frank Gonzales, Alfonso Muller, Mrs. DeZeke—the teacher
Front: Counting the boy only partially seen as one, the fourth is Joe Gonzales and the fifth is Betty Heatherly. Esther Muller, and Cecilia Gonzales should be among them. Most look so familiar, but I can't recall their names.

Picture 3, Lamy School 1952-53, Grades Pre-1st-4
Teacher Philomae Rago
Back: Rosa Chavez, Mary Lou Gonzales, Lupe Cordova, JeriAnn Clayton, Eddie Carrillo; Center: Dot (visitor), Janelle Wootton, Isidro Muller, Millie Chavez, Judy Clayton (visitor), John Joe Gonzales;
Front: Lalo and Richard Cordova, Navy and Georgie Chavez, Ricky Mares, Leo and Rudolpho Montoya
Not pictured: Ralph Gonzales, Mary Jane Muller

Philomae Rago replaced Mrs. Herrera in 1952-53. She drove daily from her home at 720 Don Gaspar in Santa Fe.

Each morning Mrs. Rago sat at her smooth wooden desk, a picture of George Washington on the wall behind her. She began with roll call, followed by a classroom pledge of allegiance to the American flag. She then assigned work to the three older classes and began with the first year students.

In New Mexico a child who turned six before January 1st was required to attend school. Education was compulsory until the age of 16. In Santa Fe County strict truant officers enforced the law. There were rarely social promotions, i.e., promoting a child to the next grade if the child did not satisfactorily complete the grade work. There were no public school kindergarten classes in New Mexico for many years to come. Rather, students did pre-first work the first semester and first grade work the second semester unless the language barrier required a full year of each. For many New Mexico students, Spanish was their first language.

Mrs. Rago called the pre-first students to sit in the little, wooden chairs near the large, warm stove. With her long pointer, she pointed to the alphabet printed on a long paper banner above the blackboard and pointed to each letter: "A says ă, ă, ă; B says b, b, b." Students repeated every alphabet letter and sound after her. Parents taught their children many things, but reading and writing was taught at school. I have heard of children who learned to read before they started school, but I knew none as a child.

Workbook pages were primarily black and white; so students could practice coloring in any subject; Mrs. Rago saw to it that we did. In addition, for every subject's workbook page, Mrs. Rago taught us to write page numbers clear across the bottom of each page and to write the words for objects on the page. Teachers were not proponents of guesswork spelling. We couldn't spell all the words by ourselves right away, but we could copy her words written on the blackboard. Blackboards were black, not green. While first year students worked, she taught other grades, one-by-one.

Every student remained seated in his own desk, no wiggling around—not that one couldn't change positions; but the schoolroom—even in schools with graded classrooms—was an orderly place so that students would not distract others. There were restroom-recess breaks mid-morning and mid-afternoon, as well as the one hour lunch break. Students were expected to sharpen pencils before class or during one of the scheduled breaks. There were times a pencil lead broke or someone had to go to the restroom; that called for a raised hand to obtain permission to get up.

In later years my mother told me it was difficult for Mrs. Rago to teach at Lamy School. Because many beginning students came from Spanish speaking homes, it was a challenge for her to provide a solid educational foundation along with a good transition to English. Not all previous teachers had had a solid command of English; so even the education of the older students had some English catching-up to do. Mrs. Rago was the type of teacher who seems to be a combination of a born educator, as well as a trained teacher. She was consistent and orderly and taught with disciplined kindness. She provided her students with educational tools and a solid academic foundation.

School began at 9 a.m.; when the teacher rang the hand held bell, students lined up and walked in together. There was no pushing or shoving and definitely no running in the halls or classroom. School dismissed at 3:30 p.m. Because Lamy was only 1.1 square mile, no one had far to walk. Our home was .9 mile from the school.

I never minded walking, except on windy days when tumble weeds blew against my bare legs—between skirt hem and socks. Also, if I had to carry a large piece of paper or tag board—poster board, the wind wanted to grab it away from me or at least bend it. I usually enjoyed seeing everything along the way. There was always something interesting to notice on the everyday path, except for a brief time when I was in first grade. One evening I overheard visiting adults say some railroaders had seen a mountain lion between Lamy Mountain and the depot. I don't remember being afraid, but I do remember being extra observant from the depot to the Catholic Church on my way to school. (Before long a mountain lion was shot at a nearby ranch.) I followed the road to the Catholic Church and then walked down the hill by Judge Salazar's house and followed the tracks until I came to the road that led to the school. At that time, most of the kids who attended Lamy School lived between the mercantile store and the school.

My sister said she seldom walked; she'd put her books in her bike basket and ride to school. When she came to Judge Salazar's hill, she'd ride down and across the tracks in front of his house. He'd come out and tell her she needed to watch where she was going; she could be hit by a train. I didn't have a bike until the summer after I finished Lamy school; so I walked. I have clear memories of attentiveness to the tracks, especially near Judge Salazar's house, not only alert for oncoming trains, but also watching the rails for rail changes, as Daddy instructed me when I was 5½. I may have misunderstood him, or perhaps I took his instruction too much to heart, but I sure watched.

If students lived close to school, they walked home for lunch; some helped with dishes or another chore while they were home. If the distance was far, students carried lunch in a lunch box or brown paper bag. Sandwiches were wrapped in waxed paper. Brown bags, lunch boxes, and waxed paper were taken back home for reuse. Those who ate at school ate at their desks, in the classroom with the teacher, and then went outside to play.

Lunches, coats, hats/scarfs, mittens, and galoshes were kept in the cloakroom. Every classroom had one. Coats were hung on hooks; galoshes were placed on the floor under one's coat. It often snowed in Lamy; so galoshes were important to protect one's school shoes because shoes were made of leather. Galoshes, made of rubber, fit over shoes and were passed down to siblings when outgrown. Snow boots would have been a luxury, but were unknown to Lamy students. Students placed their lunches near their coats or on the shelves near the doorway at the end of the cloakroom. In the one room used as a classroom from 1951-52 on, the cloakroom was the full length of the back of the classroom.

The school had two stinky restrooms: the girls on the southeast side of the building, the boys on the northwest. Paper hand towels were brown and rough. There was an outhouse on the east side of the school yard. Perhaps a previous generation of students had used that, also; I don't know.

The center classroom and the one to the east of it were used until 1951. After that only the center room of the three south side rooms was used. The class furthest west was occasionally used for a program, a craft, or a special project. Though other classrooms were unused, students could and did go in any rooms they wanted to—except girls and boys only went in their own restrooms.

Undoubtedly, at some point, someone or another had perpetrated a rumor to keep children out of the room which was separated from the others—the one at the east front which had a wood-coal cook stove. The whispered rumor was that if one went into that room, the floor or roof might cave in. Exact details were left to imaginations; but, one thing for sure, it was a dangerous place. Of course, a child must peek in—at least from the doorway—to see what such a room looked like. It didn't look dilapidated or dangerous, but we saw no reason to risk our young lives. In writing this, I found that the rumor was in place years before I started to school.

Windows in the center classroom gave students a view of the back playground, the mainline railroad track, and the hills beyond. Children could see and hear every train that came into and went out of town. Trains were no distraction; we lived with them day and night. To the left of the window wall was the cloakroom wall with a door at each end—leading into the cloakroom—and a blackboard between the doors. To the left of the cloakroom wall was the entrance door and stove wall. It had a blackboard with the large wood-coal heating stove in front—about midway. The entrance door was at the far left. It was next to the teacher's-desk-wall with its long blackboard behind the teacher's desk.

When Mrs. Rago taught, the blackboard on the cloakroom-wall was used for art and special projects. Although she let us draw, she guided us—like teaching us how to draw bricks when she let us draw a mural of the Three Little Pigs with their houses. We used colored chalk. Wasn't our art fine and colorful? Picasso couldn't have been more pleased with his work.

Each room in the school opened to the wide, window-walled front corridor, where students could gather in cold weather and play before the morning bell.

The one curious room was small compared to the spacious classrooms. It had bookshelves on two walls and a large desk. This was the principal's office. A principal? That was the curious thing to us; we only had one room of students.

There was no library, except for a few unused books on the shelves in the principal's office. Some were outdated textbooks, which Mrs. Tapia doled out to those in her class in 1954. That year the Santa Fe Library sent a book mobile to Lamy School; the book mobile introduced me to Laura Ingalls Wilder's Little House books. I enjoyed reading of her times because I lived in ordinary times.

The County Health Department must have worked hand-in-hand with County Public Schools because they visited the school, provided shots, TB patch tests and follow-up checks. We first-graders patted each other on the back and spoke highly of ourselves to one another when some third or fourth graders cried after getting a shot, and we didn't.

In addition, students received health information, like the wallet-shaped pamphlet, which advised of cancer signs. Each year students brought what dimes

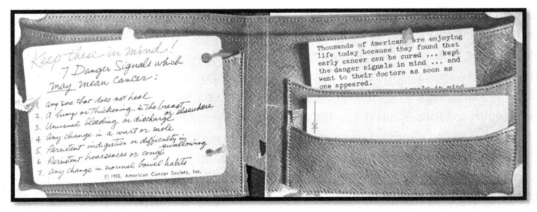

they could, tucked into the slots in their individual March of Dimes folders, provided by the county. The March of Dimes originated to benefit people affected by polio/infantile paralysis, which affected many from the 1930s until Salk's new vaccine became available in the mid-late 1950s. We didn't know all the details, but understood we were helping crippled children.

First year students had a county health and safety workbook about Dum-Dum the little donkey who didn't pay attention to safety rules. Here, he broke his leg:

Dum Dum said, "The corner's too far,

I will cross from behind this car."

We had a cross-guard in 1954-55, something the state or county instituted. They sent a shoulder sash, belt, and badge to the school. That was fine. Each student took a weeklong turn being cross-guard though all we had near the school was a dirt road, which only one student crossed, and cars seldom, if ever, used during school hours.

Many teachers taught at Lamy School before the mid-twentieth century, and others during the mid-century years; Mrs. Tapia from Santa Fe taught the longest in the 1950s. She began in 1954 and was still teaching there in 1958. Hers would hardly be a textbook approach to education. Oh, my, I don't know what you'd call it; but we learned. She incorporated play and learning—or not learning. One student who had her the year after I finished Lamy School said they went out for recess one day and were never called back in; they kept playing cowboys until they were dismissed for the day. We had no such luck when I was there, but we did have some variety.

Lamy School 1954-55:

Back: Mrs. Tapia, Eddie Carrillo, Mariquita Sanchez

Middle: Richard Cordova, John Joe Gonzales, Mary Jane Muller, Connie (Consuelo), Millie Chavez, Janelle Wootton, Lalo Cordova, Ralph Gonzales, Isidro Muller

Front: Ray Vigil, Mike Howell (cross guard, wearing badge, belt, and sash), Dot Gonzales, Lucy, Nene, Lorraine Sanchez, Leroy Gonzales

At one time, Mrs. Tapia had all the students bring empty, food cans and put them on the shelf in the cloakroom. Students of all grades drew and cut circles out of construction paper and wrote a coin amount on each. From time to time the whole school would play store: banker, storekeeper, customers, etc. I suppose that was a combination of craft and math skills, counting change. We thought we were playing. To a large degree we were; for the students themselves were the only checks and balances for the business transactions.

One day there was a funeral at the Catholic Church; we all walked with Mrs. Tapia along the short-cut path by Judge Salazar's house and up the hill to the service. We had no permission slips; we just went. Most students were either Catholic or had been to a Catholic church; so it wasn't strange to us.

On some especially snowy mornings while we stood outside waiting for the school door to open, we'd see Mariquita coming from her nearby home across the snowy lot. Mrs. Tapia had called and told her it was too snowy to drive from Santa Fe: no school today. Hooray, we had a day off! We weren't counted absent and had no day to make up. One family we knew moved from Lamy in the late 1940s because they wanted a different education for their children. They also didn't like a teacher dismissing class at varied times, like the day school was dismissed about noon when the parents had gone out-of-town during the school day.

We older girls had fun when Mrs. Tapia brought two large bamboo curtains and let us use stencils to paint designs on them in the program classroom. She told us that when her neighbor saw them hanging in her home, she wanted some like them. Both Mrs. Rago and Mrs. Tapia showed their students genuine appreciation. Perhaps we had an odd education, but it was varied with a richness of its own.

Mrs. Tapia had thick-paper pages of colorfully illustrated nursery rhymes, which she let us borrow to take home. I'd memorize the rhyme, return it, and borrow another. She didn't require it, but made the pages available. Mama had read to us since we were small, and I enjoyed the cadence of the rhyming words.

In the spring, Mrs.Tapia and Mariquita took the entire school in two sedans to a fair at the Stanley school, about 25 miles away. Stanley had grades 1-12. Some Lamy School students would be going there next year. Several older Lamy students already attended the school at Stanley, New Mexico. We drove down the two-lane highway, no seat belts—we'd never heard of them. Mrs. Tapia drove her car down the center of the highway, or a bit to the right of it—looked like center from where I sat. It would have been scary at night; but it was broad daylight, and there was no oncoming traffic. We were just going down the road to the Stanley fair.

At the fair each classroom had displays of its students' work. The little doll dresser made of matchboxes glued together and decorated looked pretty nifty to me. Any child could make one because match boxes were plentiful. People used matches for smoking, for starting fires in their wood/coal heaters, and for lighting the pilot lights on their cook stoves. Stoves didn't have electronic ignition.

We went into the gymnasium and heard the band play. One junior high school student from Lamy played percussion—weren't those cymbals fine! Of course, with the music program at Lamy School, Lamy pupils were primed to think highly of a fledgling band. We all returned home enriched and safe before 3:30 dismissal time.

Sure, we had daily work to do—arithmetic, reading, language, science, social studies. Art and music were interspersed in our days; neither seemed like an independent subject. We recorded a program with music and parts to be used on a Santa Fe radio station. The science curriculum did leave a little to be desired. No, a lot. Santa Fe County Schools provided textbooks for Lamy School; but Lamy School received science workbooks and no textbooks. Students had no source of information for many workbook questions; so Mrs. Tapia decided it would be fine for fourth graders to use third grade workbooks. No one else was using them; there was no third grade the year of 1954-55.

Near the end of the school year Mrs. Tapia and Mariquita took all students on a hike across the school yard, across the railroad tracks, and up Lamy Mountain. Everyone took a lunch.

Lamy Mountain, 2018

1954-55 was the last year fourth grade was taught at Lamy School. Here's how it happened: When Mrs. Rago taught, she wanted to be certain all first year students had a solid use of the English language. She taught pre-first to most of the beginning students all year; so their education wouldn't be hindered later. Because I already spoke English, she taught me both pre-first and first. I didn't know there was no second grade the next year because I attended second grade in Santa Fe. When I returned to Lamy in third grade, I was the only third grader; so Mrs. Tapia asked my parents if I could go into the fourth grade. My mother had finished school a year early and had no problem with the idea; so I joined the three other fourth graders. That year Lamy School had pre-first/first, second, and fourth grades in the one classroom. When we fourth graders left, there were no fourth grade students to fill our place; fourth grade wasn't offered after that.

When Lamy students completed the education offered at Lamy School, the county bused students to Stanley, New Mexico. Children had to leave early in the morning to make all the student stops between Lamy and Stanley. I don't know how early Lamy's students boarded the Stanley bus, but Dad said he didn't want us leaving for school in the dark. I don't know; perhaps it was dark at the time the bus left on some winter mornings. Several railroad families sent their children to school in Santa Fe.

Lamy students who attended Santa Fe schools waited at the depot each morning to ride the Indian Detours bus. Photo, August 2018.

Based in New Mexico, Indian Detours offered train passengers side tours for more comprehensive sightseeing, but their buses also met every incoming A.T. & S.F. passenger train in Lamy and transported passengers to and from Santa Fe—

train passengers, as well as local people who lived in Santa Fe and Lamy.

Lamy children who attended school in Santa Fe rode the Indian Detours bus to the Detours depot near La Fonda in Santa Fe. In the 1940s-early 1950s, the Detours depot was on the corner of the Plaza, directly across from La Fonda. Later it moved a block down the street, near the intersection of Shelby and East Water Street. From there students walked to parochial school at Loretto Academy or St. Michael's or to public school at Carlos Gilbert Elementary, Leah Harvey Jr. High, or Santa Fe High.

There was always a morning train scheduled at a time children could leave for school. Any experienced train traveler will understand that arriving at school on time was an entirely different matter. One day when my sister was in junior high, she didn't arrive until the second class period. Miss Breton, her music teacher, greeted her, "A dillar, a dollar, a 10 o-clock scholar, what makes you come so soon? You used to come at 10 o-clock, but now you come at noon."

I remember twice the train was so late we had to find different transportation. The first time we rode on the Branch caboose and walked to school from the Santa Fe train depot in the rail yard. In the caboose, we sat at the table awhile; but most of the time, Carmen Lucero and I sat in the crow's nest.

Another morning, short, friendly Mrs. Smith was kind enough to drive a car load of us in to town. She sat on a cushion; so she could see the windshield. It didn't really matter that she had a pillow. She was such a gifted conversationalist that she kept turning her head while she visited with those sitting next to her and only checked the road from time-to-time.

Sometimes Indian Detours sent a full-sized bus to meet a train; other times they sent a stretch-limo-size bus. The full-sized bus was like other full-sized buses at the time: two passenger seats on each side, with a full, bus-width bench seat at the back. The limo-size bus had bench seats with a door for each seat. Some mornings there would be very few on a big bus. Other times the limo-size bus would be packed full. At such times, we students would cram in together onto one bench seat. If there were siblings, the younger could sit on the older one's lap.

We saw some pretty rich people on those buses. Furs were in style. Some fur coats were pretty; but I couldn't see anything pretty about the mink stoles that had little beady-eyed heads connecting a head of one to the tail of another.

One day on the bus my sister found a wallet stuffed full of Chinese money; she turned it in at the Indian Detours depot in Santa Fe.

Most of the time we didn't mix with other bus passengers. There were enough of us to talk among ourselves, and we didn't want to be a nuisance. But one day, when only two Lamy students went to school in Santa Fe, a tourist visited with my sister and was amazed our parents would let her ride the bus that far alone. She asked if our parents weren't afraid of Indian attack.

Some years train schedules were close enough to school schedules that children could ride the bus to and from school. Other years parents carpooled. How long we had to wait depended on what time the parent got off work. There was only one for whom we occasionally had to wait a long time. On those days, I stayed in the classroom until the teacher left. When she left, the teacher let me take a class music book into the hall; so I could copy lyrics while I waited. Mr. Saiz, the janitor, was still there dust mopping the floors; I loved the smell of the oil he put on his mop. He always seemed to be on hand and kept the school warm and clean. One teacher said that during the summer Mr. Saiz refinished any desks that needed it.

Desks were made of wood on metal frames. In Lamy the desks had a lift top with storage under the top. In Santa Fe the desktop was stationary; storage was under the seat. Each had a pencil groove on the desktop.

By the beginning of the 1958-59 school year, most Lamy children who had attended school in Santa Fe had moved or transferred to school in Stanley. My sister had finished driver's education the previous school year; so that fall she

Judy and Janelle Wootton, ready to leave for school,
Fall 1958

drove my brother, friend Ray Vigil, me, and herself to and from school in Santa Fe daily. Santa Fe Public schools notified our parents they would have to pay $25 tuition per student because Stanley was the designated school for Lamy. My parents chose to move our family. Later, Santa Fe would be the designated school for Lamy students, and a public school bus would transport them to school and back.

Other Railroad Photos

Included in this section are railroad photos, which do not pertain to Lamy. All except the roundhouse photo are related to the Santa Fe Railroad.

The Santa Fe's Ginnery Twitchell
Trinidad, Colorado

A round house

133

Baldwin manufactured engines used by the A.T. & S.F.

This ad appeared in *The Santa Fe Magazine*, May 1917

The "Uncle Dick" engine was custom built by Baldwin to pull Santa Fe trains across Raton Pass, the highest point on the Santa Fe mainline. The most powerful locomotive on earth at the time, it was too heavy to cross some mainline bridges. It was shipped in parts and assembled in Trinidad, Colorado. Named in honor of Uncle Dick Wootton who allowed access over Raton Pass. Photo 1916.

The original Santa Fe depot and Harvey House in Las Vegas, New Mexico.
Photo early 1930s, at which time one floor was for storage, the other for caretaker quarters.

Teddy Roosevelt's Rough Rider volunteers board a Santa Fe train at Las Vegas, New Mexico. The train is in front of the original Las Vegas depot-Harvey House.

A.T. & S. F. Special Officer John P. Wootton, Sr., of Las Vegas, New Mexico, visiting in Lamy, in the late 1940s. Mr. Wootton was the son of pioneer "Uncle Dick" Wootton and his wife Mary Pauline Lujan Wootton.

P. S. Nice chamber pot in the yard.

A freight crew in Trinidad, Colorado, c1900-1904,
John P. Wootton, Sr. at the center

Santa Fe steam engine, Trinidad, Colorado. John Wootton. Sr. in cab.

April 1902, Santa Fe train wreck near Trinidad, Colorado

o

Santa Fe train wreck, near Trinidad, Colorado,
April 1902

Santa Fe train
wreck near
Trinidad,
Colorado,
December 24,
1902

December 24, 1902,
Santa Fe wreck near
Trinidad, Colorado

Santa Fe railroaders,
Trinidad, Colorado, c1900-04.
John P. Wootton, Sr. middle in front.

Near Trinidad, Colorado

A Santa Fe freight crew,
Trinidad, Colorado, early 1900s.
John Wootton, Sr. far right

The Day Light Crew of the A. & B. R.R. 1911

Brakeman Johnnie Wootton, Jr. unloading freight, Ribera, New Mexico, 1943

Some Mid-Century Lamy Surnames

Some of the surnames in Lamy in the mid-twentieth century are listed below. In many cases, there was more than one family of the same name. Some were related; others, like the two Mallory families, were not.

Albin	Howell	Pompeo
Anaya	Ingraham	Rumley
Belcher	Jenkins	Salazar
Blea	Jones	Samaniego
Bonney	Kirkendall	Sampson
Boyce	Koepell	Sanchez
Carbajal	Koons	Sandlin
Carillo/Carrillo	Lark	Sandy
Casick	Lehman	Scarbrough
Chavez	Lucero	Sedge
Clayton	Mahannah	Sena
Colvett	Mallory	Shearmire
Cooper	Mares	Smith
Cordova	McBroom	Stewart
East	McGinnis	Tapia
Everett	McGuire	Taylor
Goforth	Montgomery	Turner
Gonzales	Montoya	Villanueva
Green	Muller	Wootton
Griego	Ortiz	Zavilla
Heatherly	Pitt	

Resources

*A*lthough this is an oral history, written from personal knowledge and experience, I have referred to resources for some dates pertaining to Lamy's early history and to that of the Southwest Indian Detours. I have also referred to sources, listed, for seniority lists.

I have garnered historical information on the Santa Fe Railroad since my high school term paper on the subject and through the intervening years, including research done for *No Time to Quit*, which is listed below.

Bullock, Alice. *Mountain Villages.* Santa Fe. Sunstone Press, 1981.

McQuitty, Janelle Wootton. *No Time to Quit, Pioneer America Seen through the.Life of Rocky Mountain Man Uncle Dick Wootton.* New Mexico. Janelle Wootton McQuitty, LLC, 2017.

Pick, Ada. *Dum Dum.* Santa Fe. Santa Fe County Schools, 1949. Page 7.

Poling-Kempes, Lesley, *The Harvey Girls, Women Who Opened the West.* New York. Paragon House, 1989.

Railway Employees' Seniority List Time Book. Issue of Santa Fe. 1948.

Seniority Lists. Albuquerque, NM. Personal Finance Co. 1945.

Stanley, F. *The Lamy, New Mexico Story.* Pep, Texas. June 1966.

The Santa Fe Magazine. Volume X, Number 8. Chicago: Railway Exchange, July 1916. Cover.

_____. Volume XI, Number 6. Chicago: Railway Exchange, May 1917. Cover, p. 14.

_____. Volume XI, Number 8. Chicago: Railway Exchange, July 1917. Cover.

Thomas, D. H. *The Southwest Indian Detours.* Phoenix, Arizona. Hunter Publishing Co., 1978.

Photo Credits

Sources for the photos from *The Santa Fe Magazine* and *Dum Dum* are listed above.

Photos by Jack McQuitty are used by permission and noted in captions.

All other photos are the author's photography or from the author's collection.

Some Clues Remain

Information which may help those who want to search further

The United States censuses of Lamy residents provide information from 1900-1940. Reading the census reports, I found a community more than twice the size of the Lamy I knew.

In the 1930 United States Census, the station agent and the telegraph operator lived in the railroad's large duplex house next to Dr. Crume.

There was a pool hall in Lamy in 1920; Epimenio Romero is listed as working at the pool hall.

I'd heard there were charcoal ovens at Lamy or out-of-town, closer to Cañoncito and that the charcoal was shipped as far as California. I don't know the facts of that, but the 1920 census does list several men as charcoal workers. It also lists J. Neil Cox, M. D.

I had also heard there was a roundhouse in Lamy. The 1940 census lists Mindon McGee as the roundhouse foreman. Some residents listed in that census were employed by the hotel.

Carl Mares said the original school, near Our Lady of Light Catholic Church, burnt down c1920s and that his Grandpa Mares purchased the property and rebuilt the building. That may have been the same structure as the Kirkendall house that burnt down.

The U.S. Censuses add more clues to the Lamy School story. Only 33 or 34 Lamy children attended school between September 1909 and the time the 1910 census was taken. By the 1920 census, however seventy-one children had attended school since the Fall of 1919.

Having attended the spacious Lamy School with not quite two dozen students, I was amazed to find that 97-98 Lamy students attended school during the year that began in the Fall of 1929. No wonder they needed the new school. Twenty-one of those students were teens. Carl. Mares also said his father talked about playing basketball for the Lamy Lions. Mr. Mares' father would have been a teen in the 1930s.

There was a road construction camp in or near Lamy at the time of the 1940 census. The camp contributed nine students. Lamy added seventy-eight: eighty-seven students in all, thirty-three of which were teens.

Witt Harwell, who worked out of Lamy as the signal maintainer May 1952-September 1955, said that the free standing home in which the Lamy depot agent lived—listed on the map as 39—was originally built for the signal maintainer. At the time, the signal maintainer was single; so the agent and his family lived in the free standing house. From then on signal maintainers lived in the west side of the large railroad duplex house where station agent Creed had lived—listed on the map as 45. The east side of the duplex—46—remained the home of each track supervisor and his family. Although Lamy had its own water well, Witt said the railroad also had a well near Canoncito and piped water to its tanks in Lamy. Mr. Harwell later worked for the A.T. & S.F. in Las Vegas, New Mexico, La Junta, Colorado, and in the railroad offices in Chicago.

Lamy, New Mexico, 2018

The End